SECOND EDITION

REACHING
THE PEAK
OF YOUR
POTENTIAL

THE CLIMB
OF YOUR LIFE

DR. CHRIS STEPHENS

Faith Promise Publishing
10740 Faith Promise Lane
Knoxville, TN 37931

Second Edition, 2009

ISBN 978-0-9817812-2-8

Book design by Heather Burson
Cover photo © AbleStock.com
Author photo © ACapturedPhoto.com

Printed in the United States of America

"*Chris is one of the finest young leaders I have had the privilege to mentor. I have watched him grow a great church in Louisiana and now in Tennessee. Chris has been used to raise up a new generation of leaders. It has been great to watch him grow.*"

—Dr. John Maxwell
Founder of EQUIP and INJOY Stewardship Services

"*The unique life experiences that Chris Stephens shares in this book reveal that character is forged from adversity. The lessons learned and shared herein in a clear manner are priceless. Anyone seeking inspiration to reach their life goals will benefit from this book.*"

—Dr. H. Lee Martin
Co-founder and Inventor of iPIX 360 Degree Immersive Imaging System

"*The Christian life is a journey and often the steps wind upward...this excellent book will offer a hand to assist you as you climb. You can make it to the top, and Chris Stephens' message will strengthen you along the way.*"

—Dr. Ron Phillips
Abba's House Chattanooga, Tennessee

"*As Christians we sometimes confuse transformation with transportation. Our transformation from sinful to sinless is the supernatural gift of God through his Son's crucifixion and resurrection. It is free. It is marvelous. We need only to ask for this wonderful gift. The miracle does not stop here but the free ride does. The rest of the journey is all us. There are no hitchhikers in heaven. Christ requires each of us to pick up our cross and follow him. In our hastiness to explain the resurrection story we fail to mention that Christ is the way—the truth—the map—the path—not the bus. We are the bus driver. We are responsible for driving, washing, cleaning, registering, insuring, and gathering other passengers. We are Christ's transporters. Chris has captured this concept with his climb with Christ. He has taken Deuteronomy 2:3 (Ye have compassed this mountain long enough, turn ye northward) and told us to stop waiting at the base and to start preparing for the climb. In this powerful book Chris has lovingly and masterfully described both the transformation and transportation of his life. I loved it, and I am sure you will as well.*"

—Dr. Dale Henry
Founder and President of Your Best Unlimited, Inc.

Acknowledgements

How can I list a lifetime of teachers, mentors and so many others who have poured into me? There are far too many to mention, but I appreciate you all. I want to thank my wife and life-long climbing companion who blows wind into my sails daily and my three kids who have made the last 23 years exciting, not to mention giving me over 20 years of sermon illustrations. Also, to my faithful assistant who works tirelessly to help me be a success and maximize my ministry and to a host of other friends who have read and re-read this book in its various drafts and have given me countless suggestions to make it far better than I could have alone–thank you! And my eternal gratitude goes to Faith Promise Church for a great ride, our Executive Pastor who daily encourages me to continue the climb, and most importantly to my CEO and Director, The Lord Jesus Christ, who pulled me out of the bottom of the valley and carries me to new summits daily.

Contents

Introduction

    Usually people skip this part of a book but for those who don't: my name is Chris Stephens, and I'm the senior pastor at one of the fastest-growing churches in America. I started life "on the wrong side of the tracks"—abused, abandoned and nearly dead from drugs. Twenty-four years ago I had a radical experience with God. After that I started an amazing climb to reach my life's potential. The more I ascend, the more I realize we all face problems in our respective climbs, and most of them are somewhat similar. Hopefully we can learn from each other. My own mountains have taught me a lot about what works and what doesn't. I have read hundreds of books on the subject, spoken with many national leaders on the topic, studied it in schools and seminars and taught it to thousands. So I can tell you with full assurance that no matter who you are, if you really want to climb to the top, you will need help.

    This book is about our climbs and the things that will help us along the way. It includes some of the essential tools and equipment I've used in my ascent from junkie to Ph.D., from the projects to being a pastor. It's my prayer that *The Climb of Your Life* will give you a boost and help you reach your full potential.

Sincerely,

Your Climbing Companion,
Dr. Robert Christopher "Chris" Stephens

ONE

You Can't See the Top from That Far Down!

If you've ever watched mountain climbing documentaries, you realize that climbers always start from a place called base camp. A base camp is a staging area where people make final preparations for their climb, assembling their supplies, equipment, team and guides. We're all like that, in a way. We all have dreams for our lives, and from our respective base camps we get ready to face the challenges of the climb it will take to fulfill them. But there was a time in my life when base camp was nothing but a pipe dream. Reaching a peak or summit—fulfilling a dream—was out of the question.

I was 22 and very likely to die young. In fact, I'd been actively throwing my life away for the past four years. But it all came crashing down when I woke up in a dingy hospital room after a three-month binge on cocaine and Quaaludes. The doctors and nurses rushed in and out of the room and talked in hushed tones. A thin curtain was drawn between two small beds, and sounds of coughing and moaning drifted in from just down the hallway. The whole place smelled of death and illness mixed with the pungent aroma of antiseptic. I was in the far bed, a young washed-out junkie. I couldn't remember the last time I wasn't drunk, high or both. Yet the medical personnel kept checking my vital signs, running tests and trying to find a diagnosis. In place of the needle-scarred "tracks" up and down my arms were bandages, tape and tubes—trying to pump some degree of health back into my wasted body.

When my system was at last free of illegal pharmaceuticals, I was still in excruciating pain with stomach cramps that seemed to turn my whole body inside out. It could have been anything—bad drugs, dirty needles or any number of the hazards common to an addict. Truthfully, the nurses and doctors probably wondered if I was worth all the trouble. But they persevered, maybe just because I was a puzzle they couldn't solve. All the tests they could think of showed nothing more was physically wrong with me, but the pain persisted relentlessly.

As I lay in that small sweat-soaked bed all day with no visitors, friends or family, I realized I was alone—truly alone. I was also angry, frustrated and without even the dimmest hope for the future.

How did I get here? How could I have fallen so low so fast? As if to answer my own question, wretched memories of the last four years began to flood my brain. Horrible pictures. It was like watching a movie of my past, ugly scenes of violence—every blow, kick, cut or slap I ever delivered, received or watched; and drugs— the deals, money, needles and highs, followed immediately by obsessive plans for the next buzz. There was sex, betrayal and every other vile act you probably can't imagine. If there was such a thing as a living hell, I was trapped in it. Everything I said I'd never do, I did; every moral, every standard I ever had, I broke; every loyalty to friend or family, I betrayed.

Finally, I realized what being completely alone really meant. There was no one to look to, to lean on or to ask for help, comfort or direction. It was my own doing, to be sure, but still my heart, my

> IF THERE WAS SUCH A THING AS A LIVING HELL, I WAS TRAPPED IN IT.

life and my future were empty, and I desperately needed a friend. I needed someone, anyone, to help me with life because I had totally ruined mine so far.

My story is not so different from a million other addicts, but something amazing happened that Wednesday in my drab, gray little hospital room. I remembered hearing about God when I was younger. My family had not been churchgoers, but I had a friend who went. When I spent the night with him, I had to go to church with his family. There I heard about God's love, power and forgiveness. But was I beyond help? Could, would, just maybe...He might pull me out of the agony I was in? So I turned to the one Person I thought I could trust. My only hope was the only One who could reach down that low and pull me up. That day I entered into a partnership with God. I figured, what could it hurt? He couldn't do any worse than I had. Little did I know I was in for the climb of my life!

During those first few weeks and months out of the hospital, I was just happy to be alive and really had no idea what I had gotten into. I certainly wasn't going to get dressed up, sit on a church pew and sing 200-year-old songs. But I was serious about the God thing. Evidently He was serious too because it wasn't long before I realized that if God was going to be my Partner, I had better make plans—big plans. And they had nothing to do with pews and hymns.

My life changed so quickly it was like a blur. I was out of the hospital and off drugs for good. I can't explain it or give you a simple recipe for success; I just wanted to have a new life. For the first time I was actually making progress—instead of descending, I was ascending. I started attending a church and met friends that cared for me, just because, not for what I could give. I got a job and started showing up to work every day. It's amazing how you can keep a job if you show up each day. I started feeling good about myself and my future, and for the first time, I wasn't lonely or angry. I no longer felt empty or like a loser. My destiny seemed to be improving daily. I started to feel my life had a purpose for the first time, like my Partner wanted me to prepare for a life of helping others. I had been through a lot, and I began to see how it could be used for good. I started dating Christian girls, making plans, thinking of marriage and looking forward to what the future held. That's about the time groups began to ask me to speak and tell my story. People asked me to help them with wayward family members and friends. I actually saw people trapped in addictive lifestyles being freed. These new experiences gave me a reason to get out of bed in the morning.

I don't even remember blasting past base camp, but I did. I was climbing for the first time in my life. Amazingly, even better things were in store for me. Imagine, a hopeless case like me actually seeing great things happen. I found new friends, help, vision for the future and hope I had never experienced before.

As I got stronger, I began to give back, to help others get off drugs, abandon destructive behaviors and step out of defeated lifestyles. All the while my future began to look brighter and better. It was as if once I got out of the ditch, things, situations and circumstances looked better immediately. I could see my potential powerfully rising, and I began to see new heights and dream dreams I'd never dared to think I'd see. And this time it was no pipe dream.

If I may, let me ask you a question—do you believe most people will achieve their full potential? Almost everyone I ask this question answers no. Over years of dealing with people, I have learned that a person's potential is far beyond what most ever realize. I would be willing to wager that your potential is far greater than you realize or recognize, too. I'm not talking about vocational achievement or financial success, although that may be part of it. I'm talking about your wildest dreams of a rich, full life. A life of satisfaction and fulfillment and relationships. A life you can be proud of and that leaves the ones you love better because you were here. Sometimes you need someone to help you truly see your potential—a guide or mentor who can point the way, or better yet, show it to you. Who better to help you climb a mountain to your potential than someone like me who began so deep in the valley?

Now, let me ask you what I think is a far more important question. Do you think you'll ever achieve your own full potential? Think about that seriously for a moment because the question matters far more than you realize. It requires reflection and some honest thought. Your view and vision may be blocked by the storm clouds of poor choices, bad breaks or false starts, but if you let them, the skies will clear.

> DO YOU THINK YOU'LL EVER ACHIEVE YOUR OWN FULL POTENTIAL?

You may be like I was, going the wrong way; but you can get on the right path. However, I don't think you can do it alone. No one can get that far solo.

Today I can tell you that in the 24 years since I left that hospital room, I've climbed a few mountains. I'm pastor of a church that has almost 3,000 worshippers attending weekly. There are still no pews, few hymns and no dressing up. I have a beautiful wife and three nearly-grown children. The relationships in my life are plentiful and healthy. You could say I've reached my potential, or at least a large part of it. I speak from experience when I tell you that I may have started alone but that I didn't get here alone. It just doesn't happen that way.

We all need partners—friends who will run, walk and climb with us. Every successful mountain climber has a companion, a partner, friend or guide who helps him or her climb over and past the difficult parts, even when you think you can't climb another step. If you would permit me, I would love to be a "stand-in Sherpa"—a guide, if you will, to help you on your climb. That's what I'm hoping this book will be for you—an aide to help you surpass the summits that have, so far, seemed impossible to reach.

Sir Edmund Hillary was the first climber to successfully conquer Mt. Everest. He received many awards and accolades for his achievement, yet he always reminded people he spoke to that he was not the only climber and that his guide deserved more credit for the historical triumph. Like Sir Edmund Hillary, we all need help. Now, I have never climbed Mt. Everest, and you won't find my name in many record books; but I have climbed my own mountain. One of the reasons I am writing this book is that I have had so much help on the climb, such great mentors—guides that helped me navigate through the tough spots.

I've been able to help others, too, thousands of people around the world as they make their own ascent toward heights others only dream of. On my own personal journey I discovered that there were many mountains that had blocked my way. In the chapters to follow we will begin an exciting exploration into your world to enable you to climb the mountains that seem to hinder so many others from experiencing an unbelievable life.

Oh yeah, remember that day in the hospital when the doctors couldn't find the cause of my pain? It vanished mysteriously the day I partnered with God. When the pain left, I asked the doctor to release me. He simply said, "Fine," and shook his head as he signed my release. Amazing, huh? Nothing was the same after that day. It was like getting onto a roller coaster—the excitement you feel when the bar drops, locking you in, and the cart lurches forward. What a ride! What a climb!

I am no different from anyone else. I've achieved so many of my dreams, and you can too. Today can be a brand new start for you. As we walk through these pages, I believe you will find hope and help to live the most awesome life you could ever encounter. The journey to your potential will be the climb of your life!

No One Climbs Alone:
The Belay Factor

The party was on. I was 18 and out to have a great time, regardless of the cost. In those days, the purpose of life was to party, and my partying friends and I went at it with a passion, as if we were driven to gather, get drunk, high and then look for the next round of fun. That night there were three of us, Chris, Tommy and me. Chris was a friend from school, and Tommy was one of my best friends since childhood; we generally got into whatever trouble we could find. Tommy was only 12 years old the first time he got drunk. We stayed at my house so he wouldn't get caught. That night as he slept in my bed, he got sick as a dog. I cleaned up his vomit from the bed, walls and floor. It was gross, but isn't that what best friends do for each other? We were older now, but we hadn't learned much.

Everything was going great until about 3:00 a.m. We were all pretty high. I had stolen some of my grandmother's medication to provide that night's buzz. Chris provided the transportation. He had a '69 Grand Torino that resembled the car on the TV show *Starsky and Hutch*. For some unknown reason we were on a country road in north Georgia. The last location I remembered was in Chattanooga. But now we were in Georgia, and Chris was driving way too fast. I kept telling him from the back seat to slow down but he didn't listen. We all watched as the speedometer climbed higher and higher. The road had no street lights, and the curves were getting sharper. Soon it all became a blur. Chris tried to take a curve at over 100 mph. This time he couldn't hold the road, and the car skidded out of control. Had it not been happening to me, it would have been reminiscent of something out of a cheap detective movie. But it *was* real. And it was happening to me.

The final curve had a steep bank on the left side. In an instant, the car hit the bank, flipped over on its top, then back onto the road and skidded all the way down the street spinning completely out of control. When we finally came to a stop, Chris and Tommy climbed out through the broken windows. They looked into the back seat and saw me, covered in blood and with a broken neck. With no hesitation, my lifelong "friends" agreed, "Just leave him alone. HE'S DEAD!" Fortunately for me, they were wrong!

I didn't wake up until the next day, in a hospital in Fort Oglethorpe, Georgia. Every part of my body cried out in agony. While I didn't appreciate it at the time, I was lucky to be alive. This came from three guys just out having fun??? I realize now I should have chosen my partners more carefully. I guess we were all bad influences on each other.

Two thousand years ago a very wise man said, "Bad company corrupts good morals" (1 Corinthians 15:33). John Maxwell, my friend and famous leadership author, said, "The people closest to you limit the level of your success." John calls it "The Law of the Inner Circle." If you're like me, you have had some good friends or partners and some that were not so good. Give that some serious consideration because it's a simple fact that if you lie down with dogs, you come up with fleas. My friends had been close to me for years, but they abandoned me immediately in the face of trouble.

Over the years since, I have had a lot of partners who were interested in what I could do for them, and I was often interested in what they could do for me. But back then I had never had a partner who was looking out for me—one who really cared about me and where I was going.

My poor choice of partners was one reason I was descending at such a rapid rate. I guess getting drunk at 12 should have been a warning signal; but I didn't have a moral compass, and no one around me seemed to have one either. Not only was I failing to climb; I was, in fact, digging downward. It took me years to recognize that I was belayed to the wrong buddies. A belay is a safety rope that climbers use to tie the team together. If one team member falls, the others will hold him using the belay. It's a simple procedure that has literally saved thousands of lives on perilous peaks and climbs. But if you're belayed with the wrong people, you descend rather than ascend—and they may even pull you completely off the mountain with them when they plummet.

Let me tell you how it all began for me. My parents split when I was only three years old, just after my mom had given birth to my younger brother Rick. I had two step-dads in early childhood and was physically and sexually abused repeatedly as a little boy.

It made me fearful and nervous. Then my uncle gave me my first marijuana joint when I was ten years old. Please beware because there is always someone to tie onto you and pull you down a path that leads to an even darker side of the mountain.

Many of you reading this book can readily identify with me. You know the cold sting of betrayal. Maybe you were deceived, abused or worse by someone who was supposed to love and protect you. I wish my story were unique or rare, but we all know that it's lived out by millions of people every day. That's one of the reasons I wrote this book. If I can climb out of the pit to a new life with a greater purpose, so can you. There is always hope.

But back then I felt all alone. I had friends and a mother who loved me, yet I felt empty, hollow, like there was something else to life but whatever it was I didn't have it. This couldn't be all there was! I was a very angry young man when I left home at 15. The day I walked out of my mother's house was a horrible day for both of us. As kids we have no idea how badly we can hurt our parents. I can still see my mom with tears flowing down her cheeks as she said, "You won't let anyone love you." She was right. In life I was toppling down to the ragged rocks below with no safety line.

The next few years were not my best. I lived with friends, my girlfriend, and my grandmother as I finished high school. For most of those years I was drug-free and working. About the time I turned 18, I ran into an old friend Tommy. Yes, this is the same Tommy who would leave me for dead in the back seat of a wrecked car a few months down the road. But we were 18 then and ready for fun. We went out, and that was when I really started down the slippery slope. By the end of my eighteenth year, I was heavily involved with drugs. I began selling them too, catapulting me further down to destruction. By the time I ended up in the hospital in Fort Oglethorpe from the wreck, I was not only dealing drugs but I was also thoroughly addicted to them.

Now, who would have ever guessed at the time that I would climb the mountain of my potential, let alone write a book? Isn't life full of great surprises? You may have spent some time sliding down the slope yourself. You could be there right now wondering if you will ever be free to climb. I know what it's like. I felt worthless, used up and good for nothing. I had no hope the future would be any better than the past. What did I have to look forward to? The one good thing I thought I had in my life dumped me when I started getting high—my girlfriend of three years. Another shove down the dark path to the pit. It wasn't her fault; it was mine. It's almost like there is a spiritual gravity that pulls us down and tries to destroy or ruin our lives. I was playing right into its power. Maybe you have felt like I did—that no one, especially not God, would even want to be your partner. Think with me for just a minute. The Bible says, "God is love;" I believe that includes you, and I know it includes me. He has big plans for you.

God is the original big thinker. He spoke the universe into existence. He planned the sky and painted the colors of the rainbow. He invented the sunrise and the mountains. He drew the smile on the baby's face and created the sound of its laughter. He chose the courses for the rivers and set the boundaries for every beach. He designed the fish and the fowl, clouds and constellations. He patented creativity and holds the record for big ideas. Go ahead; let Him in on your thoughts. Remember, He knows your potential—*He built it into you.*

I know you want to reach the mountain peak of your potential or you wouldn't be reading this book. So let me ask you—who are your partners? Who surrounds you? Do they believe in you? Do they encourage you to soar to the next summit? Or are they like the friends I had in the beginning, looking only for the next round of fun no matter where it leads? How close will they be if there's trouble ahead?

Remember, those who surround you have the ability to make or break you. They can blow wind into your sails or be an anchor holding you in port. Take some time and make a list of those closest to you—family, friends, coworkers and teammates—people with whom you spend time. What do they whisper into your ear; is it constructive or destructive, leading to summit or slum?

This leads to my next question: do you have the right partners? Climbing mountains can be very difficult. You will need all the help you can get from people who want you to succeed. People who have your best interests at heart and have no ulterior motives or jealousy are the ones who cheer the loudest when you gain a victory.

PICKING A CLIMBING TEAM

If you've found you need a few more qualified climbing companions, let me describe ideal team members a bit further. They should be honest with you. I don't mean just truthful, but really honest. If you're about to fall off a cliff, you want someone who is willing to tell you, even if it's painful. You need people who are positive and look out for you, who are genuinely excited when you reach another summit. It's easy to find people who will climb with you when the path is level and the sun is shining. But when the air is thin, the storms are moving in and the path goes vertical—those still with you are your true climbing companions.

Also, seek out people who are further up the mountain so that you can cheer them on, and in turn they can help you. Your companions should be seeking your full potential and be willing to help you reach it. Advice from high-altitude climbers is priceless. Advice from "armchair travelers," those who have never been where you are, is not as valuable. It is amazing to me the number of people who seek out known failures for help with their marital problems, financial issues, major life decisions, etc.

For the last six years I have toyed with, thought about and struggled with writing this book. My climbing companions have steadily encouraged me to complete it. They have read it, re-read it and helped in a multitude of ways. Authors like John Maxwell, Ron Phillips, Dale Henry and Lee Martin have had a major influence on me. All are successful and busy like me, yet they love to see other people succeed. These are the kind of climbing companions you need.

You may be connected to some negative people in your life. They will drain all your energy and then blame you for failing to reach the top. They will discourage you and continually throw cold water on your red-hot ideas. Some of these negative people you can—and should—avoid. However, others you cannot. Some may be your relatives; others may be your work associates. They simply can't be avoided.

You have to be very careful at this point not to believe everything people say about you, but at the same time, don't confuse constructive criticism with negativity. Climbing companions must be able to share truth even when it's negative. The difference is that their hearts are for you, and their overriding motivation is to see you succeed. Other people really are just dead weight. They don't plan to climb and are very happy if they can get you to stay with them at the bottom. Ask them if they believe in you and if they think you have great potential. If possible, don't allow negative partners to remain in your sphere of influence.

Let me ask you another question: are you a positive companion to those with whom you come in contact? Do you blow wind into the sails of those around you? Do you encourage them to great heights and big achievements? Do you push them to trust and have faith in themselves? To have great companions, you must be a great companion. You have the option to speak life or death into their lives—so please speak life! Remember the Golden Rule, "Treat others as you would have them treat you" (Matthew 7:12).

When your life is over, will you have reached your full potential? I don't know my ultimate limits, but it gives me great comfort to know I will not be judged by anyone's potential but my own. I remember a story I heard years ago about a man who came home from a hard day's work. His first son met him at the door with his report card. By the smile on the boy's face, his dad could tell the news was good. Straight A's! Wow, his dad was proud. Wouldn't you be?

"Jeff, how did you get that algebra grade up?" As he asked the question, the dad also noticed his other son, John, on the floor at his feet. John was severely challenged mentally, but he couldn't wait to show his dad what he had learned at his school that day. The dad sat on the floor with John in their usual position. He watched with utter amazement and joy as he saw John tie his shoe for the very first time. Tears filled his eyes because he was so proud of both his sons. He didn't scold John because he couldn't read or compare him to his brother Jeff. Their potentials were entirely different, but both brothers were judged and rewarded according to their own abilities.

So how are you doing? Are you gaining on your potential? I believe your potential is at an extraordinary altitude. As a matter of fact, it is so awesome that you can't reach it on your own. That's the reason for this little book. I hope you receive some encouragement and practical help in clearing the hurdles you'll face on the climb to your potential. Look around you; who is on this journey with you? With whom are you soaring to your summit? Are they people who encourage you and believe in you?

I remember my first day in Greek class as I was working on my Master's degree. The professor asked the question, "Who has 20 hours this semester?" I raised my hand. "Who is weak in English grammar?" Again, my hand went up. "Who has never studied a foreign language?" My hand again. "Who is working a job along with seminary?" Guess who? Again, I slipped my hand up. The professor looked at me and said, "You can't pass this class. You need to go drop this class today." I don't believe he'd taken any Dale Carnegie courses in positive communication skills! Despite his advice and to his ultimate surprise, I passed the class (partially to prove him wrong) and later graduated with honors.

You can climb like that too, no matter what "the professors" in your life are saying. Your potential is undoubtedly well past where you are today. Don't listen to the naysayers who are going nowhere and want you to stay with them. You can soar with the eagles. My Spiritual Sherpa is always encouraging me. I hope you likewise find encouragement on every page of this book. Remember each chapter deals with one seemingly unscalable, sheer-faced barrier that tries to discourage you from being your best. It helps you discover how to overcome that barrier. There is always a way.

> DON'T LISTEN TO THE NAYSAYERS WHO ARE GOING NOWHERE AND WANT YOU TO STAY WITH THEM.

No one ever achieved greatness alone. Your potential is too high for you to achieve it by yourself. If you look around, you might be surprised at all God has planned for you. Trust me, if God can take me from the depths of despair where I started to where am now, what could lie ahead for you? I believe God has even more than we can imagine in store for both of us. He wants us to soar and reach great heights.

- Remember the belay factor.
- To whom are you tied? They could save your life.
- Be careful who is on the journey with you. They may either help or hurt, but few are neutral.
- Beware who picks your peaks.
- Remember that you choose whom you will allow to speak into your life and what you believe about yourself.

You can climb high regardless of how low the valley is where you began. Your past is not your future. What you can be is far more important than what you have been. Your past can be a launching pad instead of a prison. It's up to you.

Do the people closest to you believe in you? Who is cheering you on to greater heights? Who could lend you some faith?

No one achieves greatness alone. No one climbs alone—the journey is too dangerous. Choose carefully who will be your climbing companions.

Are you willing to help others to a higher elevation? You be the cheerleader for those around you. There are too many people out there telling them they can't make it; don't join them. Never let yourself or others be labeled a loser. God didn't make any losers!

God can and will climb with you if you ask. In the 24 years since I walked out of that hospital, I have climbed higher than I ever dreamed I could. God has big plans and if He is your Partner, you had better get accustomed to big plans.

Seize the Summit!

It's so easy to lose faith. There are always points along the path to our potential that feel like the end of the journey. The summit is so steep we simply can't go on. Have you faced circumstances you thought were insurmountable? Without question, you probably knew there was no way around them. It probably felt like a dead end, but please don't lose faith—there is always a way to make it up the mountain. Let me tell you what happened to me as I stared up at a summit that seemed impossible to scale.

In the months after I walked out of the hospital in Chattanooga, I had a different take on life. I had a burning desire to help people. Imagine going from being a drug dealer where it was all about me to actually wanting to help others. Trust me, it was quite a transformation. My life and influence were expanding rapidly. Several groups had asked me to tell my story of abuse and addiction to help others in the same situation. My confidence grew, and with some encouragement from others, I decided to go back to college. Four years earlier I had flunked out because of my tendency to smoke dope before every class. That's not a good strategy for keeping your grades up.

My biggest problem now was finding the money to go to school, but I took a deep breath and applied for re-admission to the University of Tennessee at Chattanooga anyway. At the time, I didn't know how I would even meet my living expenses, much less pay for school. They admitted me on academic probation due to my first failed college experience.

I scraped up every dime I had which was about $400.00, barely enough to pay for the first semester's matriculation fees totaling $393.00. That was a lot of money back then. Just before the semester started, I went to the bursar's office to pay my fees, and waited in a long line. As I stood there in that sea of people, I wondered what I was going to do and how I was going to live. Was I doing the right thing? This had to be nuts. Negative thoughts began to surface and nearly took over my mind. I thought of leaving, but for some reason I stayed in spite of my fears and doubts. When I got up to the cashier, she asked my name and rummaged around in a thick stack of papers for my bill. (This was B.C.—before computers!) She found it, pulled it out and handed it to me. There was a simple note attached. "Your fees have been paid by an anonymous friend. Good luck." I was shocked! Totally speechless. When the message finally registered in my brain, I yelled out loud and started laughing and dancing around the room. I still smile when I think of it now. Everyone must have thought I was crazy! But it was a miracle as far as I was concerned. It was just the first in a long line of many extraordinary events in

THE UNIVERSITY OF TENNESSEE
AT
CHATTANOOGA

OFFICE OF THE BURSAR

MEMORANDUM

Date: 8/18/82

To:

From: *Robert your fees have been paid by anonymous friend. Good luck Sue Rucker*

my 24 years with a phenomenal Partner. I never found out who paid my fees, and I will never forget the lesson I learned. So I kept this receipt to remind me that miracles can happen at any time.

Have you ever experienced a miracle? A miracle is an extraordinary, unexplainable event in your life. They occur around us every day. What if I had not started school because I was afraid of the finances? What if I had given in to my doubts and fears instead of waiting in line for the cashier? That day I learned a valuable lesson to help me on life's journey. The lesson is that without faith and trust you will never make it to the top. Doubt and fear come easily, but you have to work at faith and trust. This is one of the first hurdles you must jump in order to run the race to the end.

For many brave enough to begin this amazing journey of potential, it will seem as if you are beginning to climb a mountain, just like starting college was for me. You have your own Mt. Everest staring right at you, daring you to climb it. If you don't have the faith that you can do it, you will never make an attempt. The bad news is that your potential is not even at the top of that initial mountain. Oh, you'll climb it, learning lessons and gaining strength along the way. But that mountain is just the first in a range of mountains you must climb to reach the pinnacle that has your name on it. Once I was preparing to give a

> IF YOU DON'T HAVE THE FAITH THAT YOU CAN DO IT, YOU WILL NEVER MAKE AN ATTEMPT.

series of talks about mountains and those who climb them. I used an ancient scroll of wisdom called the Book of Zechariah. The author was speaking for my Partner when he said: "If it is too difficult in your sight, it will be too difficult in My sight" (Zechariah 8:6, paraphrased). Even though this quotation is 3,000 years old, it still packs a powerful punch today. This lesson is too important for us to miss. Basically, it says if you can't see it—God won't do it! I have heard

> "IF IT IS TOO DIFFICULT IN YOUR SIGHT, IT WILL BE TOO DIFFICULT IN MY SIGHT."

John Maxwell state it more positively: "If you can see it, you can seize it." For us to win any war, we must first win the battle in our minds and hearts. I love how Winston Churchill put it: "The empires of the future are empires of the mind." As Prime Minister during World War II, he saved Great Britain because he believed they could defeat Hitler. You must believe you can climb the mountain in front of you, and each one that comes after it. Look up to the summit and know you will reach the top.

When I first stopped doing drugs, all my old friends laughed at me. They constantly told me I would fail. It wasn't long before each

of these friends detached himself from my belay rope. They found
me no fun anymore, and I found them extremely dangerous. Every
time they saw me they offered me drugs,
in an effort to pull me back down into the
pit where they lived. They didn't believe
I would stay clean and remain on the new
road I was walking, but they were wrong.

> "THE EMPIRES OF
> THE FUTURE ARE
> THE EMPIRES OF
> THE MIND."

Remember earlier I said that when I was in the pit it was as if
there were a spiritual gravitational pull on me? Ever since I made
God my unseen Partner, the pull is now reversed. Whereas I was
being pulled down, now I am being pulled up. Up is so much better
than down! Take it from me; I've been pulled both ways. What
made me different from so many others who tried and failed to stay
clean, to get right, to climb up instead of falling down? It was my
help from my new Partner. My old friends had never seen anyone
get and stay clean, so they didn't think I would be the first. They
were wrong and still are. Most importantly, I did not believe my old
friends' expectations of my failure. I knew I would make it because
I believed I could. It is called faith! Faith is "the assurance of things
hoped for, the conviction of things not seen" (Hebrews 11:1).

Faith deals with things unseen, and the future is as unseen as you
can get. Do you have faith that your future will be great? Do you
expect good things to happen to you? Can you see things working
out for the best? I expect the best, and I am usually not disappointed.

After I graduated from the University of Tennessee at Chattanooga—thankfully debt free—I moved to Memphis with my wife
Michele and our new daughter Faith where I went to seminary
to get my Master's degree. After graduation I took a position as

pastor at a small church in Jennings, Louisiana. It was a small town in the southwest corner of the state. We found ourselves deep in Cajun country where it is said the state bird is the mosquito. The small church had about 25 adults when we arrived. The church was young and didn't really have a vision. For this reason and so many more we could have turned this opportunity down. Not the way most think one should start a career. No building, no vision, no money, but Michele and I believed God had a plan. Remember, you must have faith and trust that the future will get better.

We arrived in Jennings looking like the Clampetts in *The Beverly Hillbillies*. We pulled into town with a U-Haul truck that was towing two cars, all of them loaded down with furniture and everything we owned. By this time we had added two sons to our brood, Micah and Zac. We called them the Sons of Thunder. As we pulled into the driveway of our rental house, all we had was zeal and faith in a great future. I discovered the town of Jennings was in the *Guinness Book of World Records* for having the most churches per capita of any city in America. There were churches everywhere, but almost all the churches were small and had little vision for the future. But we would not be discouraged. Most of the other churches had fallen prey to small dreams, tame vision and colorless lives. They did not think they could impact the small town, but my Partner had bigger plans.

Remember, you are only as strong as what it takes to stop you. We had faith and hope, and no one could steal it. Author Orison Swett Marden said, "All men who have achieved great things have been dreamers." Not many years earlier I had dreamed of staying clean, of getting a college education and then a seminary degree.

Now it was time to dream again. My Partner won't let me sit down for long. We all need rest, but far too many stop and never get up and get going again.

The little church called Bethel began to grow. People from all over town began to pack the small building. We only had 10 parking

> **REMEMBER, YOU ARE ONLY AS STRONG AS WHAT IT TAKES TO STOP YOU.**

spaces and room inside for about 75 to be seated comfortably. Soon the 25 adults we started with had grown into 100 people trying to crowd into its four tiny walls. It was hot, muggy and very uncomfortable. We only had two choices: build additional space or quit growing. Having experienced so many miracles along the climb, I had become an incurable positive thinker, so you can guess my decision. We were on the move!

We found some property and started a building project. The project seemed impossible for the little church; faith was a must if we were going to reach our potential. At one point during the construction I realized a spiritual dimension to a physical dilemma. It was a question of trust. My friend Keith Wall rang my phone at 6:00 a.m. He was helping with the construction, and it was time to pour the concrete slab; but the weatherman was calling for rain. Keith asked me what to do. Send the crew home and try again tomorrow, I told him. But as I lay back down in bed, I felt badly about my decision. I had not even consulted my Partner before giving my answer. I just handled it. But I got a second chance to make the right decision. The next day the same scenario played out. This time when the phone rang at 6:00 a.m, I was ready. Keith asked the same question, and I told him I would be right there. As

I pulled up, the crew was waiting. The weather report said 100% chance of rain. It was raining 20 miles west and heading in our direction. How much faith did we really have?

I asked the foreman how long he needed the rain to hold off. He said if he poured the slab he needed dry weather until 9:30 p.m., but he said there was no hope. He pointed west and said a storm was coming. I told him I had faith, and I believed it would not rain until that night. I told him to pour the concrete. He said he would not be responsible if the rain ruined the floor. I asked him if he would come to church if it did not rain until 9:30 p.m. Even though he was not a "churchgoer," he said he would be at church if the rain held off because he thought dry weather that day was impossible. I'm sure he also thought I was crazy, but I knew it was time to step out...and if I got him into church at the same time, so much the better. He reluctantly agreed to pour the slab. At 9:31 p.m. the rain fell. On Sunday, the foreman was "front row center," and everyone was amazed at yet another miracle. Faith is always a powerful tool in our hands and hearts. "With God nothing is impossible."

What barriers are blocking you right now? What would you like to do that seems impossible? Faith unlocks the impossible. I have seen it so many times in hundreds of lives and families and in a multitude of circumstances. What should have

> FAITH IS ALWAYS A POWERFUL TOOL IN OUR HANDS AND HEARTS.

happened didn't, as with the rain. What should not have happened did—wayward spouses that came home and money that arrived just in the nick of time.

But we live in a negative world. There is always someone to tell you why you can't reach the summit and why you shouldn't even begin the climb. That's why I always try to keep positive people around me and read positive books to reinforce my thinking. One such book I read was called *Positive Imaging*, by Norman Vincent Peale. It was a gift from a senior adult friend. It was pretty old, but a treasure nonetheless. Basically he taught that you first get a picture in your mind of how things should be. Then you believe it and work toward it. Your mind will "make it happen."

Let me explain how the concept works and how you can apply it to your life to build your fantastic future. Every day I spend time with my Partner. In my time with Him I look forward to our weekend church services. I visualize every service filled to capacity. I see our overflow sanctuary also filled. In my mind I see thousands of happy, excited people growing in their relationship with God. I see them growing and helping to change our community in positive ways. I see new faces and new people meeting God for the first time. I keep their images in my mind and look forward to it all week.

For my kids I do the same thing. My daughter is 22, and my two boys are 18 and 20 years old. I look forward and imagine them living a great life. I see them as happy, well-adjusted adults, achieving their full potential and doing great things for others. In the distant future, I even imagine beautiful grandkids. Author James Allen said, "You will become as small as your controlling desire or as great as your dominant aspiration." I plant thoughts of greatness in my kids. I believe we are all destined for greatness—that is, if we are willing to climb the mountains that appear unconquerable.

Many people who come to our church are in deep trouble. They are consumed with problems involving drugs, lust, alcohol, money and greed, to mention just a few. I pray for them, and I visualize them overcoming—becoming healthy and happy. I see their marriages and finances restored and see them set free from problems that would destroy them. That is the image I get in my mind for them and for you.

> "YOU WILL BECOME AS SMALL AS YOUR CONTROLLING DESIRE OR AS GREAT AS YOUR DOMINANT ASPIRATION."

What precipice are you facing? What do you need desperately right now? Physical healing? Financial resources? Family rescue? Relationship restoration? What would it be like if you received a miracle? How would your life change? Now get that picture in your mind—the picture of you climbing to new heights. Keep the picture there, and ask God to help you see it happen. Remember, "If you can't see it, He won't do it" (Zechariah 8:6, paraphrased).

I have a very close friend whose name is Chuck Carringer. He is the principal for one of the top high schools in the United States. His wife Emily is on our staff. They have two beautiful kids, Zach and Maggie. A few years ago they noticed Maggie was having mild seizures. By the time she was diagnosed with Generalized Absence Epilepsy, the seizures had increased to hundreds daily. Even so, little Maggie was always smiling. The whole church began to pray for her. Today, Maggie has started second grade and has fallen behind in school due to the seizures. I spoke with Chuck the other day. He told me he has already prepared his story to share with the church the day she is healed. Emily, his wife, is making a list of all the people who have prayed for Maggie so she can send thank you notes when Maggie has her last seizure. They continue taking her to doctors and specialists and keep her medicated, but daily they also trust their miracle will come. It would be easy for Chuck and Emily to give up or get discouraged. Obviously they have hard days; but they close their eyes and see little Maggie seizure-free, and they trust.

Author J. G. Gallimore said, "Image creates desire. You will be what you imagine. Seeing all possibilities, seeing all that can be done, marks the power of imagination. Your imagination stands as your own personal laboratory. Here you can rehearse the possibilities, map out plans and visualize overcoming obstacles. Imagination turns possibilities into reality." John Maxwell puts it this way: "If you embrace possibility thinking, your dreams will go from molehill to mountain-sized, and because you believe in possibilities, you put yourself in the position to achieve this."

No successful mountain climber ever started the journey to the top of a mountain believing he or she would not make it. I believe you can reach the top of your mountain. You must believe it yourself, for yourself. Today is the day to develop a can-do attitude. Your attitude will give you wings to soar, or it will be your anchor, always holding you back. You may have heard it said before, but it's worth repeating:

Your Attitude Determines Your Altitude!

- You have to see the summit before you can seize the summit.

- Miracles happen every day. Never give up because your miracle could be just over the next apex.

- You must see it if you are going to climb it. Too many people never climb because they don't believe they can reach the top—they sit at the bottom of the mountain and miss all they could achieve.

- Many will attempt to slow your ascent. On my climb I have had many try to steer me off the path. They were not going to climb, and if I did, it would make them look bad.

  "YOUR ATTITUDE DETERMINES YOUR ALTITUDE."

- Expect good things to happen. Murphy's Law was repealed. You will receive what you expect, so expect the very best.

- Paint the picture in your mind of the top of the mountain, and work toward the peak. We all have an image of what the end of the climb will be like, so paint an awesome view. Even if you don't make it as far as you planned, you will be farther than most. Often, I have heard Zig Ziglar say, "There are no traffic jams on the second mile."

- Believe it will get better. If your circumstances are difficult, please believe they will change for the better. They will change and what you believe may come true. Pastor Robert Schuller said, "Impossibilities vanish when a man and his God confront a mountain."

- Believe you will make it to the top. No climber starts the trek up the mountain believing he or she will fail. Faith is a gift from God, so ask Him for it in abundance!

The view is amazing at a higher altitude. I have interviewed many high climbers and read hundreds of their books. They all agreed the climb was worth the effort and the view was unbelievable. You must believe the climb is worth it or you will not complete it. Can you feel the pinnacle calling your name?

FOUR

Vertical Limit

As I write this chapter, our brave armed forces are fighting in Iraq and Afghanistan. You may have heard the story of professional football player Pat Tillman who volunteered to fight for our country. He had just signed a $5 million contract to play for the Arizona Cardinals, but he considered the war a more important assignment. Sadly, he lost his life early in his tour of duty. As the news anchor reported his death, she called it "friendly fire."

This was not the first time I had heard the term, but I had never contemplated the real meaning. When I heard the explanation that it meant being shot by someone on your own side, I was deeply saddened. How can you shoot your own man and call it friendly? What an oxymoron.

Yet when you think about it, we are all hit by friendly fire from time to time. The friendly fire I'm talking about is worse than being shot by someone on your own side. These bullets come

THE CLIMB OF YOUR LIFE

from your own gun. I'm not just talking about the shock we share when someone has turned a gun on themselves, although that's part of it. I'm talking about how we all shoot ourselves with words, and that these wounds can do even more lasting damage than bullets or other weapons of destruction.

> THE BOTTOM LINE IS THAT YOU ARE EITHER A VICTIM OR A VICTOR! YOU GET TO CHOOSE!

Too many people allow "stinking thinking" to sabotage them from reaching their full potential. Like a camouflaged enemy combatant or an undercover mole, we usually don't recognize stinking thinking even when we choose it. At least not at first. But we all choose our attitude and how we think. You may not be aware of having made that choice, it's so automatic. We typically choose by default and not by deliberate decision. This means that if you want to root out stinking thinking and its negative impact on your future, you must make it your new responsibility to learn to recognize it. Then when you catch yourself knee-deep in stinking thinking (again), stop and make a better choice. Stop blaming others for your problems, attitude and mindset. Accept the responsibility for your thinking today, and start living the change right now. How you think, and not what happens to you, is what will determine whether you are a victim or a victor! You get to choose, regardless of your circumstances and surroundings.

> WITHOUT QUESTION, YOUR THINKING, DETERMINES YOUR VERTICAL LIMIT. HOW HIGH CAN YOU GO?

Without question, your thinking determines your vertical limit. Now, how high can you go?

44

I remember when I came to East Tennessee to visit a new church called Faith Promise. They asked me to pray about becoming their pastor. During my second visit I met with the Pastor Confirmation Team, four members of the church whose job it was to find a suitable leader. During the interview I shared my life's story of sexual and physical abuse, drug addiction—the whole story. I can still remember watching the mix of shock, concern and compassion on the faces of Bobbie and Nola, the two ladies on the team. "Chris, have you had counseling for your past?" they wanted to know. I laughed and told them how my Partner had healed my scars and my thinking. My past was no longer a prison but a launching pad to a great future. My previous life was left behind at the bottom of the valley, and I had soared far past my past. I have learned that you can't climb very high carrying weight from the past.

As I share my journey, please don't think I'm degrading good Christian counseling. I have seen hundreds helped along the climb by good counselors, friends and pastors. If you are stuck on a precarious ledge, PLEASE get help. Remember, no one climbs alone. Those that try to climb alone typically don't go very far or high, and many end up falling. If you keep your backpack filled with problems from the past, you will most certainly not reach your potential. If you are carrying a heavy load, allow someone to pull garbage out of your pack.

Far too many people have what I call a "lottery/lawsuit" mindset. They are waiting to win the lottery or a lawsuit, and then life will get better. They think that one day their luck will change, or their ship will come in almost by magic. John Maxwell calls it "destination disease." It's just another aspect of stinking thinking—an attitude that says I'm not going to change but my life will get better. If that sounds familiar or in any way true of your thinking, then I have a reality check for you. It's summed up in the old adage, "If you always do what you've always done, you'll always get what you've always gotten."

As a pastor to thousands, I watch so many who stay stuck with stinking thinking—almost like a hamster on a wheel—running but getting nowhere. Many really hope to wake up one day to a better life. If you are in what I call a "cycle of sin," it won't go away or get better on its own. You will have to make a change and put forth some serious effort. Make the decision today to get on the path to a better life. My Partner can help!

> "IF YOU ALWAYS DO WHAT YOU'VE ALWAYS DONE, YOU'LL ALWAYS GET WHAT YOU'VE ALWAYS GOTTEN."

Today, make a decision to start thinking correctly. We all know that "you will reap what you sow" (Galatians 6:7). Start planting seeds of good stuff in your life and the lives of those around you. Your harvest will be great. Reading this book is planting good seeds. Today you're the result of seeds you've sown in the past, and in the future you'll be the result of the seeds you sow now, which is what makes this "Partner Principle" so important in everyone's life.

Let me give you a 3,000-year-old word of wisdom. "As a man thinks within himself, so he is" (Proverbs 23:7a). This is so true. The number one factor that determines whether or not you reach your potential is how you see yourself—how you think.

I know it's hard to believe that it could be that simple, but it is. I have talked to many people with problems who tell me they

46

are going to move across America, hoping things will get better. I usually tell them that won't work. Wherever you are, there YOU are. The way you think of yourself when you live *here* is the same way you'll think of yourself *there*. You can't move away from yourself.

> THE NUMBER ONE FACTOR TO DETERMINE IF YOU WILL REACH YOUR POTENTIAL IS HOW YOU SEE YOURSELF—HOW YOU THINK.

Think of it this way. If you think you're a loser, you will be. I see it daily. If you have a poor self-image, you will subconsciously sabotage yourself to stay in line with how you see yourself. But the reverse is true as well. If you see yourself as a winner, your mind will go to work for you rather than against you. As a man thinks, so he is.

I have watched many single women try marriage many times with the same results, a bad ugly divorce. Usually these relationships were filled with unfaithfulness, abuse and neglect from the husbands. Why the same story,

> IF YOU HAVE A POOR SELF-IMAGE, YOU WILL SUBCONSCIOUSLY SABOTAGE YOURSELF TO STAY IN LINE WITH HOW YOU SEE YOURSELF.

same song and same results? The women didn't think they deserved better, so they married the same kind of man. It all flows out of how you see yourself.

As you start monitoring your thoughts for stinking thinking, be aware of the potentially blinding power of expectations. When I was 14, I was riding my motorcycle down a main street and noticed a car stopped at a cross street stop sign just ahead. I had the right of way. The woman at the stop sign looked straight at me, eye-to-eye and proceeded to pull out directly in front of me. She left me no road or any place to go but down. I locked up my brakes and went into a power slide. I came off the bike and slid right into her door. As this happened, she glared out her window at me as if I had done something wrong!

Why did she do that? How could she see me yet not react appropriately? Because she was looking for a *car*. She expected to see a *car*, and because she didn't, *she saw nothing*. The fact that I was there, riding a motorcycle with the right of way, didn't register with her mind at all. We normally see only what we're looking for, even if something (or someone) else is right in front of us. The power of the mind is extraordinary. This is the reason stinking thinking is so dangerous and potential-limiting.

Stinking thinking is one of the main reasons so many will miss their potentials. I have heard it said that for most people it's not what they are that holds them back, it is what they think they're not. Thomas Edison believed, "When people have hope, there is no telling how far they can go." Paraphrasing President Calvin Coolidge, author Dennis Waitley wrote, "The winner's edge is not in a gifted birth, a high IQ or talent. The winner's edge is all in the attitude, not aptitude. Attitude or thinking is the number one criterion for success. You can test for IQ, for strength, ability and for many other factors, but not for attitude. Just wait and watch; those with good attitudes will rise to the top. It really is your choice—of thought, attitude and expectation. Pure and simple."

As far back as I can remember I was fearful and depressed. I was afraid of my "rageaholic" step-dad, and that fear spread eventually to color my whole world. I had been sexually and physically abused by the time I was 11. I had no positive male role models as I was growing up, and I had never seen a marriage that didn't end in divorce. How could I have an optimistic outlook for the future with a past like that? I didn't say it was easy, only that it was possible and absolutely essential. Then I offer my life as evidence. If I can change my thinking, then you can too, so get started today, now—from this moment forward!

When I was growing up, the only positive people in my life were my mother and grandmother, but their influence was eclipsed by the rest of my world. By my 13th birthday all my friends and I were sexually active and experienced drug users. We lived in the impoverished section of town where harmful people and lifestyles were easily accessible. I was fully engulfed in stinking thinking. For the next nine years life went downhill fast. Had I not met my new Partner at 22, I'm convinced I would not be alive today. I'm grateful He had bigger and better plans for me. How I fought His plans when I was younger. I can remember wanting to quit drugs and leave the misery, and I could feel God drawing me out of the mess I was in. But I didn't listen. Why bother? I knew I was trapped with no way out. If I went to bed without being high or drunk, or without a girl, I would cry myself to sleep. I hated my life. I didn't recognize God's help. Today I am so grateful for my unseen Partner and that He never gave up on me.

> "A SHALLOW THINKER SELDOM MAKES A DEEP IMPRESSION."

Once He placed me on the right road, He had to change my thinking. There's a saying that "a shallow thinker seldom makes a

49

deep impression." Since my Partner had all these big plans, I had to develop big thinking to match. Slowly He moved me from negative to positive thinking. It took some work and time. But the more I learned about God, wow! The world seemed to change. It didn't really, but I did—at least my thinking and focus. God brought a series of great people into my life. One of these people was my first spiritual sherpa, John Yarbrough. What a help John was for me as I began my climb. He took me under his wing and began to show me what a father was really like. He taught me how to share my faith, read the Bible and communicate clearly the message of hope.

Since my Partner's plans for me continue to be so amazing, He still works on me and my thinking today. Once I'd shifted my thoughts from negative to positive, He began to give me dreams and visions for my life that were unbelievable. They were so huge that I was scared at first. I didn't dare to tell people about them for fear they'd laugh at me. No one else I knew seemed to be thinking that big. The more I read the ancient text of wisdom, the more God tampered with my dream life. How's your dream life? What do you see in your future?

I'll never forget the first time I realized my church in Jennings had such a limited vision of what was possible. We had petitioned a group of local churches in the parish (that's a county for you non-Cajuns) for membership. A group of church leaders and I met with the Director of Missions from the association of churches in the area.

The gentleman in charge asked me if we were going to be a community church. I told him no. He asked if we would be a citywide church and I also answered in the negative. Everyone in the room looked puzzled. I told them because Jennings had only 11,000 people, we would be a regional church. We hoped to reach out to the whole parish of 32,000 people. We wanted to see people coming from the north, south, east and west. I told them my Partner was going to build a great church.

After the meeting I was shocked to find the men who had come with me were upset with my presentation. "How could you tell him that?" they admonished. "Tell him what?" I asked. "That we would be a regional church! How prideful! Where did you get an idea like that?" I was speechless. It was at that moment I realized they had no vision. A small and shallow dream life had taken root in their hearts. They had planned to do what they had always done and get what they had always gotten. Growth, particularly aggressive growth, was just not in their plans. So I had work to do to share my vision. At that time we had only about 50 people attending the church. When our family left six-and-a-half years later, we were the largest church in the parish with over 500 in attendance weekly. No church in the parish had ever grown to that size. On our last Easter weekend in Jennings, 3,200 attended in seven services because the church began to embrace the vision.

My vertical limit of thinking continued to increase to the point that it scared me. Just how high could I climb? That's when God placed a second mentor in my life, John Maxwell. Oh, he had mentored me before we met, through his books, tapes and seminars. He not only gave me permission to think big but also showed me how to harness big thinking and climb. I had been listening to John for three years when in 1993 I heard he was going to be in Houston for a conference. His student pastor was a friend of mine in San Diego, so I asked him to tell John I was going to say hello at the conference.

Now I'd been to many conferences and I knew that the speakers usually didn't spend time with attendees; but I introduced myself to John and asked if he had any free time or meals I could schedule with him. He agreed to a breakfast meeting the next morning at his motel. I spent hours that night getting ready for our meeting. I had pages of questions. I wouldn't waste a minute of his time or my opportunity. I could hardly sleep.

Two men from my church, Ray Boudreaux and Keith Wall, went to breakfast with us. Bill Clausen, John's prayer partner, was also there. I was so nervous I couldn't eat. For an hour I fired questions at my hero. As I saw our time was coming quickly to a close I asked John to pray for me, and he asked what I wanted him to pray for. I told him I wanted to build the greatest church since Pentecost. The next 30 seconds are burned into my mind. "Bill, did you hear what this 'boy' wants?" Fear gripped my mind. Now I've done it—I've made him mad. He thinks I'm arrogant. My stomach knotted up—good thing I hadn't eaten. Then John's face lit up. "Come on Bill, let's pray for this boy!" Nothing fires up a leader like vision and big thoughts! I knelt in the middle of the restaurant. John and Bill laid hands on my head and both prayed for me. I sobbed! I didn't care if people watched. I could feel the Favor of God settling down on me. Wow—what a day! Do you want Favor? Ask for great spiritual leaders to pray for you.

> NOTHING FIRES UP A LEADER LIKE VISION AND BIG THOUGHTS!

God was not through with me, and He still isn't. He leads me to books, CDs, seminars, mentors and experiences to grow my thinking. He's not finished with you either. He is continually stoking up the fires of positive thinking! He has to because there are so many ready to put out the fire with their wet blankets, shallow thinking, small visions and tame dreams.

The more you learn of God the more your faith and positive thinking will grow. Today, 24 years after meeting God in the hospital, I have seen so many miracles it's unbelievable. Now it's easy for me to think positively, but it hasn't always been. Life is an awesome journey, and He continues to transform my mind. Remember your thinking can either be your vertical limiter or your enabler.

SIMPLE STEPS TO STOP STINKING THINKING:

Make A Decision To Change Your Thinking. Start acting on that decision today.

Take Responsibility For Your Attitude. "Your attitude gives you altitude." I am a private pilot. In my plane there is an "attitude" gauge. It shows the attitude, or pitch, of the plane. If the gauge is negative, I'm going down. If the gauge is positive, the plane is going up. It is the same in your life.

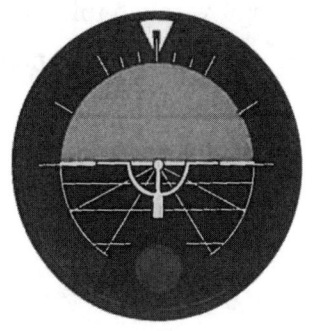

Set Up A Personal Growth Plan. (More in Chapter Nine— Strategies for the Summit) For now, just start writing down your thoughts, even the scary ones.

ATTITUDE GAUGE

Saturate Your Mind With Good Stuff. Sow positive seeds with books, CDs, seminars, friends.

Get Rid Of Negative Influences, If Possible. Remember, if you lie down with dogs, you come up with fleas. Put the dogs in your life outside.

Find An Accountability Partner. Give him/her your growth plan. Meet and pray weekly. Encourage each other.

Set A Daily Meeting With Your Partner. And never miss your appointment.

Commit For The Long Haul. This is a way of life, not a quick fix. You didn't get where you are in a day. Change requires time.

Expect Results. Celebrate every win. You must allow yourself to celebrate all God does in and through you. Celebrating will give you the impetus to work toward the next win.

Help As Many Other People As You Can. Most of us have no idea how much influence we have—or can have—on others. Speak words of life and encouragement, and do all you can.

Is Your Base Camp in Order?

As you look down the valley, you can hear the wind whistling through the pine trees. The sky is a beautiful blue with wisps of white clouds floating by like sailboats on the ocean. Most of us have hopes of life looking something like that—all sublime and peacefully perfect. We all want some version of this happy life, and most of us also think we know all the pieces necessary to achieve it. Things like health, money, friends, family, success, faith...and you could probably name several others. For the serious climber, one of the essential elements is your base camp, your home. Everyone wants to be painted into a Norman Rockwell scene, no matter what his or her present circumstances. If your home is wrecked, your life is at least for the moment derailed, and your potential will be severely limited. With whom would you celebrate at each new summit? Your base camp is vitally important.

We in America compartmentalize our lives into divisions such as work, recreation, physical fitness, spiritual life, etc. Some aspects of our lives may be able to stand alone, but your base camp affects everything else, without exception. Just imagine for a moment how hard it is to succeed at work if you just left World War III at your house! The first institution ever created was the family. Before there was business, government, school or church, there was family. It even pre-dates the Fall of man in the Garden of Eden. So you can imagine that we should know a few things by now about what makes families work and what doesn't.

> IT IS HARD TO SUCCEED AT WORK WHEN YOU JUST LEFT WORLD WAR III AT YOUR HOUSE!

Right now, your family may be a total wreck, or maybe you've been through a bitter divorce. Regardless of your circumstances at camp, it can change for the better. If God is your Partner, you should expect your home to be a sanctuary not a storm. He's willing to help you achieve the support, peace and sanctuary you need in your base camp. It takes time and work, but it can happen. Even for you.

I remember reading a leadership book, *Leaders: The Strategies for Taking Charge*. I was surprised by something the authors Bennis and Nanus uncovered. They had interviewed ninety very successful business leaders in order to uncover some unknown or overlooked common keys to leadership. "The only surprise worth mentioning is that almost all were married to their first spouse. And not only that, they were also indefatigably enthusiastic about marriage as an institution."

You and I may try to compartmentalize our lives by using DayTimers, PDAs and the like, but our minds simply don't work that way. Your home life is your base camp, and its quality will affect your enjoyment, achievement and performance in every other area of your climb.

I have a friend who was once living life in the proverbial "fast lane." He was a successful business owner with money and a family, but he also indulged in alcohol to excess and was involved with other women. You probably know about how well that worked out. His family started to unravel, and his business started to collapse as well. He was losing everything. During a trip to his sister's house, he heard someone talk about God as a potential Partner. He was desperate. Grasping for help, he reached out to God. About a week later, we were introduced for the first time. We began meeting so I could help him with his newfound faith. I met his estranged wife and their five sons. As time passed, his wife saw almost unbelievable changes in her husband. They reconciled, his business turned around, and today he is more successful than ever. God is still his Partner and has even blessed them with a beautiful new little girl after five boys!

The truth is that businesses can go bad, we can go broke, we can lose our health, and many other areas can fail. But as long as the family is okay, we can weather the storm. When the family falls to pieces, so does everything else.

So how do you make your base camp strong and stable? The first step is to make sure your Partner is welcome. Since He invented the family, He knows best how one should function! A little help from the Manufacturer's Handbook (otherwise known as the Bible) wouldn't hurt. Since your Partner is pro-family, He'll help you regardless of how bad the past may have been. My life is a prime example of the fact that your future doesn't have to look like your past, especially if God is involved. Even though when I was growing up I never saw a marriage that lasted, I have been married to the same woman for 23 years. And after all that time I can still say with confidence that my wife Michele is the most awesome person I know. I have told Michele many times if she ever left me I was going with her.

On our first date we talked about what we were looking for in a spouse. As the relationship developed, we sensed God at work. We both felt His hand bringing us together, but neither of us said a word. In the months that followed, we married and made God the center of our new base camp. As we started our new life together, we made some serious commitments to each other and to God. These were our commitments:

FUNDAMENTALS FOR OUR FAMILY

- God is our unseen partner and climbing companion
- We are always a team
- Problems push us together and never apart
- We never use the word 'divorce'
- We always enjoy life
- We honor each other

Throughout the years we have made many other commitments, but these have helped us stay close even in times of storms. Let's go over them a little more in detail.

God Is Our Unseen Partner And Climbing Companion

What kind of partner can make a full contribution if you totally ignore them? No one. And since God's favor can't rest on us if we push Him aside, this first fundamental is non-negotiable. That means we must have some knowledge of His advice! Things like, "Don't let the sun go down on your anger" (Ephesians 4:26) and "Husbands love your wives so much you would die for them" (Ephesians 5:25, paraphrased). "Forgive each other or God won't forgive you" (Matthew 6:15). "It is not good for the man to be alone" (Genesis 2:18). "Husbands, love your wives and treat them with honor so your prayers aren't hindered" (1 Peter 3:7). In the early years of marriage we almost never fought. I thought it was because we had a perfect marriage. It took me years to realize we didn't fight because Michele wouldn't fight. I just about always got my way. That sure makes life good for one person, but not for the other who gives all the time. As I grew in my faith walk, I realized Michele was getting the short end of the stick, and I started giving and considering her feelings more. Life got better for both of us. I guess I forgot there are two people in a marriage. It's easy to focus on yourself—actually it is human nature—but to focus on your spouse, now that's more like it.

Rick Warren, author of *The Purpose Driven Life*, said at one of his conferences, "The family is like a garden, a place to grow people." That means everyone in the family. Young, old, girls, guys. I've seen a lot of domestic violence and abuse, and unfortunately, women bear the brunt of it. God didn't make women to be whipping posts. He gives them a place of great honor. He even has a lot to say about sex, but we'll save that for a later book. Don't forget that God invented sex. I think it was a stroke of genius.

To have a happy home, make God your Senior Partner and live as He directed. His instructions weren't intended to keep us from fun but to protect us from failure. Remember, I lived my first 22 years as the world says. It was about me and what I wanted to do. My fun, my way, no matter what the cost. I promise God's plan is better and more fun. From the world's perspective it doesn't make sense, but my home is an awesome place to be. It is even the hangout for our kids and all their friends. As a Father, He always looks out for our good. The more we obey Him, the more He is able to bless us.

We Are Always A Team

Teams always climb higher and have more fun than individuals. I have watched many couples that were not teams. The marriage makes a team just like a sports team. If you know the coaching career of Phil Jackson, it's easy to see he is a winner and so are his teams. Remember, he coached the Chicago Bulls with the great player Michael Jordan. Jackson knew that a team was not about one player; it's about what the group can do together. I have watched teams that are filled with "superstars" that can't ever win the big game. Superstars are playing as individuals and are worried about their personal stats and how they look in the game. You can hear it when they blame their teammates after a loss. I have seen superstar mentalities so many times in marriage. The two never seem to become one. Many couples have separate checking accounts and credit cards. They got married, and instead of merging two lives into one, they kept separate lives. "The two shall become one flesh" (Genesis 2:24). Needless to say, those marriages rarely make it. Most marriages don't if the individuals that make up the couple don't work out how to become a team working together. "Two are better than one" (Ecclesiastes 4:9).

When Michele and I married, she quit college and I finished. When I went to seminary, she worked full-time, and I worked part-time until we had our second child. Then she stayed home. I worked full-time and went to school full-time. It wasn't easy during those early years, but we were a team with a common goal. We made decisions as a team and worked as a team. We were broke and had three small children, but we were a team. As I look back, all the trials Michele and I experienced drove us together. We were broke, busy and focused on the future. Most of the time our parents were not near us, so we only had each other and our Partner for help. We had dreams of changing the world, and we had a lot to do to prepare for that. It was amazing how God provided during those years. I have heard, "What doesn't kill you makes you stronger." It's usually said as a joke, but those early years put steel into our spines, and like training camp, the trials we faced prepared us for greater challenges. As we grew stronger as a team, God used us in greater roles. It was amazing.

Problems Push Us Together And Never Apart

My background as well as my early ministry gave me a chance to witness a number of marital disasters. What I noticed is that most couples argue over the same types of problems: money, sex, kids, decisions...the details may vary a bit, but the fights are essentially about all the same things. I decided that when I got married, problems would push us together rather than apart. Instead of money making us fight each other, together we would fight and conquer the financial challenges we faced. Together.

I've seen the same dynamic work with a couple in our church, Bill and Mona Rowland. Mona was diagnosed ten years ago with cancer. After her second bout with the disease, her doctor gave her less than two years to live. They were determined to fight this crisis together. Mona went through some very harsh treatments and still does. Her husband Bill cooks, cleans and cares for her. He has stood by her side all the way. He has prayed and believed she will be healed. Now ten years later, she is a miracle—not yet fully healed but still alive, and we believe one day she will be fully healed. Once, over 100 people from our church went and surrounded her house. We held hands and prayed for God to spare her life and heal her. So far He has answered our prayers, keeping her alive against all the odds. Bill and Mona are a team. This "problem," huge as it is, drives these two together, not apart. They derive much strength at base camp.

We Never Use The Word 'Divorce'

If you have been through the tragedy of divorce, please keep reading. I am not going to load you with guilt, but if you re-marry you need to be ready. When Michele and I got married, we agreed that divorce wouldn't be an option—murder maybe, but never divorce! Why start out like that? If we were committed to stay together, we would both work harder to resolve whatever issues came up.

That doesn't make it easy; we have had some highs and lows, but we have the security of knowing that, God willing, we will always be together. Why would I leave my best friend, number one cheerleader, lover and mother of my children? There is no one I'd rather spend time with. No one cares for me more or believes in me more than Michele. God said, "He that finds a good wife finds a good thing" (Proverbs 18:22). Well, mine is the best.

Early in our marriage I was very critical of Michele and didn't realize what a jewel I had. Being an obsessive-compulsive personality can be hard on your mate, and I was no exception. Journaling helped me turn the corner on criticism. Every day I would write my prayers. Part of my prayer time was spent in thanksgiving, so daily I would write what I was thankful for. I would thank God for my wife, among many other things, and list her great qualities. Daily the list grew. The more I thanked God for Michele, the more I loved her and the more grateful I felt for her. My eyes were opening to how awesome she really was. She even noticed my change in attitude. What was a good marriage was moving toward great.

But it takes work. I love Michele and pray for her daily. I want to help make her dreams come true. Now many years later I still thank God for Michele and list the many things I'm grateful for about her. Some days God gives me such love for her it hurts. She is a gift from heaven. Remember, when base camp is intact you can face the hardest slopes of the mountain, especially when your spouse is cheering you on.

An angry husband went to a wise marriage counselor. He told the counselor his marriage was over and he was filing for divorce. The counselor told the man he should do just that, but not yet, for he would lose much of his money in a heated court case. Instead, he suggested that he wait and trick his wife. Every day he should tell his wife how much he loved her, how grateful he was for her and list several good things about her. Then when she was unsuspecting, hit her with the divorce papers. By the time she got over the shock it would be over. Three months later the counselor saw the man and asked him if he had filed for divorce yet. The man replied, "Are you crazy—and lose that great woman?" Speak kind words, and don't allow divorce into your vocabulary.

We Always Enjoy Life

This should be a goal for every couple. It helps if either the man or woman is *sanguine*. That's one of several different personality types and is the one that is the most fun-loving, party-waiting-to-happen type. It's useful to know your personality type and that of your spouse because it helps you know and prepare for your natural strengths and weaknesses and how to balance each other. There are several good books on the topic. I am a *choleric*—a take charge, driven, Type A personality. Michele is a sanguine. Even though I am only 46, she calls me "Papaw" because she's always ready for an adventure or a party and I'm always ready for an intense time of planning and problem-solving. She makes life fun. God said, "Laughter does great like a medicine" (Proverbs 17:22) and "The joy of the Lord is our strength" (Nehemiah 8:10). God really wants us to enjoy life. "I came to give you life and to give it to you abundantly" (John 10:10). If I get too serious or concerned, Michele is always there to make a joke about the situation. By getting me to laugh, she helps me recover the right perspective. We should never take ourselves too seriously. Take God seriously but not yourself. Michele continues to help me learn to laugh at myself. Camp is more fun if there is laughter.

We had an older couple in our church in Louisiana. He had gone blind, yet they still enjoyed life together. She painted, and they were both very active in church. One day I remember his telling me he had driven the 15 miles to church. "How?" I asked. She replied, "He stuck his cane out the window and felt for signs!" They loved life and each other, and their base camp was a great place to be.

As you can imagine, we have many struggles in church work. Yet we have a blast! When was the last time you had fun with your spouse? Loosen up and live a little!

We Honor Each Other

Have you ever been around another couple that fought and continually put each other down? After an evening with folks like that, you and your spouse are likely to be fighting as well. Negativity and conflict are contagious, so be careful with whom you spend time. It's essential that you honor the people in your camp.

I'll never forget a story that changed my attitude about honoring Michele. I was in San Diego playing golf with John Maxwell and Dick Peterson, who was president of John's company, INJOY Life, at that time. I was in the cart with Dick. I asked him a very personal question about John: *was he the real deal*? Dick told me a story about being in the office with John when Margaret, John's wife, came in. During her time there, John and Margaret had a disagreement. John immediately deferred to Margaret. In essence Margaret won the issue. When she left, Dick asked John why he let Margaret win.

John's answer spoke volumes. "Dick, I love my wife, and she adds such value to my life that I NEVER have to win an argument." To put it mildly I was speechless. Not only

> "...I LOVE MY WIFE, AND SHE ADDS SUCH VALUE TO MY LIFE I NEVER HAVE TO WIN AN ARGUMENT."

did I realize John's true character but even more valuable was the lesson on how to treat my wife. In honoring her I never have to WIN. Honor your spouse and your base camp will be blessed.

I always try to honor Michele, especially in front of our kids. I tell my daughter, "Marry a man that treats you like I treat your mom." I also know that because of our family life my boys have a model to follow when they get married. God says to honor each other. Then He is free to let His favor rest on our homes.

Years ago they had a great custom for weddings in the Netherlands. The young couple started the wedding ceremony at the home the man had built. Once all the guests had arrived at the home they exited out the side door to go to the ceremony. When the wedding party was out of the house, the groom nailed the door shut. This symbolically closed the door to divorce. Years later when one of the couple died, the funeral started at home. The side door was finally pried opened and the casket was carried out for the funeral. This was the first time the door had been used since the wedding.

Make the wise choices in life and marriage with your words, actions, attitudes and choice of friends. I get such joy and love from my family—it is the way God designed it! It is His plan for you. Even if things are not great, God can help. Get some counseling. Spend time with good Christian couples. Read Gary Chapman's book, *The Five Love Languages.*

We all know that the family is of supreme importance. Yet many of us work harder in other areas of life that we all readily admit are not as important. You can fail at business and be happy. You can experience physical setbacks and still have joy. You can fail and get up and keep going, but if your home is a wreck all the other areas don't seem to matter. Where is your focus?

I have seen God heal marriages, restore love and return hope. He is able—do you believe? What fun is it to reach the top of the mountain and watch the view all alone? What would it profit a man if he gained the whole world and lost his family? Yes, your potential is so great you can't achieve it alone. You will need your family—your base camp—to get there, stay there, enjoy the climb, and savor the view.

If you get tired and weary in the climb, look to your loved ones at base camp. In ancient days kings often went to war. If the outcome was in question, the king would call for the women and children.

> WHAT FUN IS IT TO REACH THE TOP OF THE MOUNTAIN AND WATCH THE VIEW ALL ALONE? WHAT WOULD IT PROFIT A MAN IF HE GAINED THE WHOLE WORLD AND LOST HIS FAMILY?

He would place them in a spot where they could be clearly seen by the warriors. The king would call to his men in battle and point to their families. "That is what you are fighting for." Many times a badly beaten army found renewed strength to fight and win. Many a battle was turned around at the sight of loved ones. They are why we go on. Keep the fight, the faith and the climb; you'll be glad you did.

SIX

What If I Fail?

Several years ago I got a call asking if I could speak at a five-day conference in Colorado. It would be in Winter Park, a great ski resort. I could spend all day skiing if I would speak every night. Now, I had never been snow skiing, but it sounded like great fun. The first morning I went to the mountain with some of the conference attendees. They were all experienced skiers and assured me I didn't need any lessons, they'd all help me out. So, off we went up the mountain with our freshly rented skis and equipment.

I got off the lift and immediately fell down into the snow, backing up all the rest of the skiers trying to get off the lift. Then all my new friends who had been so encouraging started down the mountain, leaving me at the top clueless of what to do next. Finally I found some folks I thought I knew and reminded them I had never skied and they were supposed to help me. They said it was easy, just point the skis down the hill and enjoy. I was sure there was more to it than that and pressed them for more help. Oh yeah, they asked, you do know how to snow plow, don't you? NO!!! I don't know anything. Never skied, no knowledge, terrified! After a few much-needed pointers, we were off to the GREEN slopes. Hours later I was at the bottom. Even as terrifying as it was at times, I have to admit it was a blast.

Today I love to ski—both on water and snow. I learned to water ski as a child and snow ski as an adult. It may have been less painful learning as a child, but there were more lessons to be learned as an adult. As with most aggressive and driven personalities, I thrive on improvement, progress and even competition. So as I learned to snow ski, I noticed an odd correlation between my falling down and improving my new ability to ski.

Initially this didn't make much sense because good skiers don't fall, or so I thought. Finally I realized that I fell down when I pushed myself or tried something new. As long as I didn't

> I NOTICED AN ODD CORRELATION TO MY FALLING DOWN AND MY IMPROVING ABILITY.

attempt anything, I never fell down. At that point I learned a very valuable lesson. Falling or failing is a part of growth and success! To get better you must fail. This revelation revolutionized my climb. It enabled me to attempt to scale slopes in life I thought were impossible. I could now try because falling or failing is okay.

Do you see failure as friend or foe? Your viewpoint will bring your potential closer or move it way out of reach. Strange as it may seem, failure is on your side. Sounds shockingly strange, huh? It is your ally not your enemy. This "Partner Principle" is huge if you are to reach your full potential.

As most of us know, Michael Jordan is arguably one of the best basketball players in the game. What you may not know is Michael was cut from his high school basketball team. He was not good enough. I would call that a failure—but obviously for him it wasn't final. Listen to what Jordan said about failing: "I've missed more than 9,000 shots in my career on the basketball court. I've lost almost 300 games. Twenty-six times I've been trusted to take the game-winning shot and missed. I've failed over and over in my life, and that's why I succeed." Jordan's past was a launching pad not a prison cell. It can be the same for you.

Brian Tracy, noted author and speaker, said, "Failure is an indispensable prerequisite to success. It is how you learn the lessons you need." You can either learn from your failures or internalize them and stop climbing—just quit. Many people develop a stronghold of insecurity. Their stronghold won't allow them to attempt something at which they could fail, or (heaven forbid!) make a mistake. This puts their potential clearly out of reach. I hope this doesn't describe you, but if it does—

> "FAILURE IS AN INDISPENSABLE PREREQUISITE TO SUCCESS. IT IS HOW YOU LEARN THE LESSONS YOU NEED."

it's time to grow! Your Partner will help if you open up and ask Him to help you change and stretch beyond your comfort.

SEVEN FACTS TO FACE FAILURE

1. Failure Is Not About You

Failure doesn't define who you are. We already covered the dangers of stinking thinking in Chapter Four. Wake up; choose for yourself what enters your heart and defines who you are. Far too many people with great potential internalize their failures and allow them to devastate their futures. If they were to fail again, they would feel even worse about themselves, so they never risk anything again. They're truly stuck. But failure is never final unless you allow it to be.

"Only those who do not expect anything are never disappointed. Only those who never try, never fail." I heard this quote years ago; and it helps me because I've failed many times, yet I realize I'm not a failure. I choose to believe the failure is not about who I am but about what not to do next time. As the pastor of a large and growing church, I have to hire many staff members. Over the years I have made some very "poor" hires. Just because I failed at some hires didn't make me a failure as a pastor. I just try to learn from my many mistakes and keep going.

Ice skating legend Kristi Yamaguchi didn't internalize it when she fell down during the 1992 Winter Olympics. The crowd gasped when she hit the ice. What would she do with no chance to win after a fall? She jumped up with a smile at the crowd and went on to win the gold. She knew falling was a part of skating. Failure is there for us all, but it is not who we are. So we must see failure as our friend.

2. Failure Makes A Fabulous Teacher

Thomas Edison never seemed to worry about his thousands of failures. He said each failure showed him how not to do something. He learned what didn't work and continued forward, never the worse for wear. Since you and I live in a generation of innovation and creativity, we probably will climb some hills rarely traveled. As we traverse in new ways, we will make mistakes. We will learn and keep going—that's what successful people do.

Almost everyone knows it was Moses who went to Egypt to free the Israelite slaves. Most forget that 40 years earlier he tried the same task and failed. Remember, the movie with Charleton Heston as Moses? He killed an Egyptian soldier in order to free the slaves. He was discovered and fled as a murderer and a fugitive. It wasn't until 40 years later when he returned after the burning bush experience that he succeeded in freeing the Jewish slaves.

If you look deeply enough, you will find it is the same way with most successful people in almost every area of life. According to a Tulane University study, "entrepreneurs fail in an average of 3.8 business ventures before finally making it." Thomas Watson, founder of IBM said, "The way to succeed is to double your failure rate." If you are not failing, you are not trying and stretching enough.

It's tempting to want to put as much distance as possible between you and your mistakes, but if you want to learn from them, you must face them squarely and ask the right questions. Asking questions of your mistakes and those of others will keep you learning, growing and soaring to your full potential. Some questions to ask yourself:

"THE WAY TO SUCCEED IS TO DOUBLE YOUR FAILURE RATE."

What caused the failure?

This may sound obvious, but what went wrong? Did it have to do with a lack of experience, resources, expertise, judgment? What could have made a difference in the outcome? Evaluate your mistakes with the future and your potential in mind.

Am I going to fail forward?

Failing forward is getting up and doing better, learning from your mistakes. Since you will have to get up and try again—what was good about it? What can you celebrate? Are you still alive? Okay, let's go on.

What life lessons can I learn?

To learn, you must evaluate. Since I speak publicly several times a week, I have made many blunders. One time while in the middle of a message on giving, I wanted to communicate the thought of total participation by the entire congregation. I said to a full church "You can have the full Monty." I thought the term meant "go all the way" as in giving with your whole heart. I didn't realize it meant naked. So I basically told the church that if they all gave, we could all get naked! Fortunately, most of these failures aren't fatal, and we all have a great laugh. One of my worst faux pas was in a talk to a group of teens. I was talking about living in a condominium when I inadvertently used the word "condom" instead. Now try to be serious with a group of high schoolers when you have just told them they could grow up and live in a condom! While my mistakes have been funny and plentiful, I've learned through them what not to say, what jokes not to tell. I have learned how to connect with an audience and how to move their hearts. Without question, every failure has taught me a lesson and made me a better speaker.

Who can help me overcome my failures?

Depending on what kind of failure you experience, you may need help. Every successful person has had help. Most weren't afraid to ask. Get a book or CD in the area of your failure. I promise you that for every mistake you make someone else has already made it and has generously shared how to overcome it.

What's next?

Stop? Quit? Never! In 1998 Mark McGuire set a new baseball record with 70 home runs. The more times he swung for the fence, the more he struck out. One hundred fifty-five times during the season! You will never hit a home run without swinging for the fence. No one hits home runs sitting around waiting to win the lottery. Swing away! You will strike out. It's okay; just ask Mark. Author William Ward summed it up when he said, "Failure should be our teacher, not our undertaker." Failure is delay not defeat. It is a temporary detour not a dead-end street.

> "FAILURE SHOULD BE OUR TEACHER, NOT OUR UNDERTAKER."

3. Drop The Blame Game And Leave The Moan Zone

Have you ever noticed that people act like failure is avoidable? It really isn't, but since they believe it is, they will do anything to try to avoid it. When this group fails, they start the blame game—it's not my fault. They will make a million excuses and never accept responsibility for the failure. Others will move into the moan zone, griping and complaining about everything. It may alleviate your feelings, but nothing positive can happen. Never accept excuses or join in with whiners. Admit the failure and say "I'll do better next time." Learn, grow and soar on.

Jim Russell was a pastor on staff at the church I serve. He oversaw all of the children's ministries. He never played the blame game or entered the moan zone. When Jim made a mistake or failed, he came straight to my office. Before I could confront him he told me exactly what happened and how he blew it. He owned it, apologized and asked me what to do about it. How could I "fuss" when he faced failure? He did not make or accept any excuses. He continued to learn from failure and was a valuable part of the senior team. He made many mistakes—but haven't we all? Own it, punt out of the moan zone and move to a better field position. I have used Jim as an example to my kids and even to the church at large.

4. Don't Fear Failure—Face It!

One of the most famous football coaches of all time, Vince Lombardi, said, "The Green Bay Packers never lost a football game. They just ran out of time." You hear that and get the idea that his tongue was firmly planted in his cheek when he said it and that he would make sure they didn't often "run out of time," at least not for the same reasons. Actor Mickey Rooney quipped, "You always pass failure on the way to success." It's true. We would all be higher up the mountain of our potential if we just faced failure. Remember, failure is on your side. So when he knocks at the door, and he will, don't ignore him. Let him in—face him—and show him the back door, but don't let him leave until you've learned his lessons. He will be back as long as you are advancing toward your dreams and your potential.

> "THE GREEN BAY PACKERS NEVER LOST A FOOTBALL GAME. THEY JUST RAN OUT OF TIME."

John Maxwell said, "Failure is either your friend or your enemy—and you choose which it is. If you play a dirge every time you fail, then failure will remain your enemy. But if you determine to learn from your failures, you actually benefit from them—and that makes failure your friend." Let's choose to face failure head on. English author William Bolitho wrote, "The most important thing in life is not to capitalize on our gains. Any fool can do that. The really important thing is to profit from our losses. That requires intelligence and makes the difference between a man of sense and a fool." We all know failure well—just face him.

5. Get To Know Failure—He's A Part Of The Climb

Since Adam and Eve made the first colossal failure in the Garden of Eden, we have all followed in their footsteps. It's a part of the human condition. You can no more reach your potential without failing than you can take a road trip without fuel in your car. Mistakes are just a natural part of the journey we call life. What you do with these failures will determine how close you come to your potential. There is no way around it, so I suggest you accept it and embrace it.

President Theodore Roosevelt was a winner, yet he faced many problems, failures and setbacks. He said, "Far better it is to dare mighty things, to win glorious triumphs, even though checked by failure, than to rank with those poor spirits who neither enjoy much nor suffer much because they live in the grey twilight that knows no victory or defeat." If you are to achieve your potential, as Roosevelt did, you must get to know failure—and embrace it as your friend.

Do you know anyone who has never failed? Jesus Christ is the only person that comes to my mind. That means all successful people, and even those who miss their potential, fail. I believe the successful embrace it and live life to the max anyway. Failure is my friend—we've been together often.

In 1915 Ty Cobb, the great baseball player, set a record with 96 stolen bases that year. He made 134 attempts. That means he was thrown out 38 times. Maybe his record would have been higher if he had tried more often. Seven years later Max Carey got second place in the record book with 51 stolen bases. Amazingly, he was only thrown out twice. 96 out of 134 vs. 51 out of 53. Carey came up short 36 fewer times than Cobb—yet Cobb held the record. What if Carey had tried more often? What if he had been less cautious? What about you? What failures do you need to attempt again?

6. Focus On The Prize—Not The Problems

Every day you and I choose our attitudes and our focus. If you are going to achieve your potential, you must focus on the prize. If you keep your eye on problems, failures and mistakes, that's all you'll see. According to John Maxwell, "Successful people are not afraid to fail, but they keep their focus on the prize. They develop the ability to accept failure and continue on. They realize that failure is a natural consequence of trying. The law of failure is one of the most powerful of all the success laws." This idea has been around for a long time, but it is no less powerful. Eighteenth century British journalist Nelson Boswell said, "The difference between greatness and mediocrity is often how an individual views a mistake." Those who achieve their potential focus on potential not pitfalls. I told my wife Michele to have inscribed on my tombstone, "At least he tried."

J. M. Barrie, the Scottish author of Peter Pan fame said, "We are all failures—at least, all the best of us are." John Maxwell wrote

> "THE DIFFERENCE BETWEEN GREATNESS AND MEDIOCRITY IS OFTEN HOW AN INDIVIDUAL VIEWS A MISTAKE."

a great book on the subject, *Failing Forward*. In it, he asserts that one of the greatest attributes of a leader is to fail forward. We must expect it yet keep our eyes on the peak not the valley. You can only hit what you aim for, so aim for the prize.

7. Never Accept A Failure As The Final Word

Have you ever seen anyone give up? I have seen many. They just stop trying, get discouraged, and some even commit suicide. But failure is never final until you quit. You are only as strong as what it takes to stop you. Failure never has to be the final word. I have re-married several couples who have divorced, only to get back together. The divorce was not the final word.

Never surrender, no matter what you're facing now. With God's help you can overcome. He said if you have "faith the size of a mustard seed (that's small) you could tell the mountain to move and it would" (Matthew 17:20). I have watched people come out of some deep pits and terrible circumstances. Never surrender to your circumstances. If you are under your circumstances—it's your choice. The final word can be your full potential.

Failure is one of the major roadblocks keeping people from realizing their full potential. But it can also be your shortcut to the summit. Remember, that things are not always as they seem. You may have seen Mel Gibson's movie, *The Passion of the Christ*. On Friday Jesus was crucified, a horrible death. All His followers lost hope—all their visions, dreams and hopes died on the center cross. Peter went back to his fishing business. They viewed the cross as the most colossal failure in history. That was Friday.

Sunday came as usual—we call it Easter. Some of Jesus' female followers went to visit His grave. They went to mourn the "failed"

Jesus. At the grave they were confronted by an angel. He asked them, "Why do you look for the living among the dead?" (Luke 24:5). They didn't understand. Even though Jesus had told them exactly how He would die and rise again, they still missed it. Then they witnessed the no-longer-dead Jesus make His first post-cross appearance. The ladies were shocked, and they ran to tell the rest of His disciples. They didn't believe the women's report. It's so easy to believe bad news and so hard to grasp good news. Later Jesus presented Himself to the disciples and dispelled any doubt. In case you forgot, that event split time in half and changed the landscape of the modern world, but at first everyone thought His ministry had ended in a dismal failure.

How do you see yourself? What, if anything, are you wringing your hands about? Is there a failure that you believe has destroyed your future potential? It could turn out to be your best asset. It all depends on what you do with it. Let your failure catapult you to the next level and on to your full potential.

SEVEN

Acquiring an Apex Attitude

We have an awesome children's program at our church; there are hundreds of kids every weekend. There was a time when our brave Children's Pastor occasionally took them off campus. One such time he had them away for kids' camp, and he asked me to drive up and spend the day with the kids and workers. Off I went on a beautiful two-hour drive in the Smoky Mountains. (I love my job!) When I arrived, I found the Children's Pastor's cabin, but he wasn't there. Instead, I met Cory, a ten-year-old boy who taught me a big lesson about attitude.

I had never met Cory, so I introduced myself. As is my custom, I went over to shake his hand. Much to my surprise, rather than shaking my hand with his, he offered me his stump of a leg, holding it out for me to shake. Until that moment I hadn't even realized he was missing a leg! For a split second I wasn't sure what to do. Cory snickered with an infectious, mischievous grin.

This was a new experience for me, but obviously not for Cory. He waited for me, his little stump hanging in mid-air, so finally I grabbed it and shook it. "It's great to meet you," I said. He seemed delighted I'd played along with his prank.

That was my first experience with this wild, exuberant ten-year-old. I had to find out more about him, not because he was missing a leg but because I was so amazed at his awesome attitude and wonderful sense of humor. Information about Cory was easy to access. All of our children's workers knew and loved him. They all commented about his amazing attitude. As I'd surmised, I wasn't the first person who shook his stump, and I'm certain I won't be the last. He has too much fun watching people's shocked faces. It's guaranteed to break the ice, putting everyone around him on notice that he's perfectly at ease with the situation. There will be no pity parties for Cory. Recently I talked to his step-mom about his attitude. She said many people ask about him. Here is an excerpt from an e-mail she sent me:

> "...Because this was his condition from birth, it is normal for him; in fact, he runs circles around most people— and that with just one leg! Though Cory has an obvious handicap, it is not the first thing that you will notice about him. If you are the average person, the first thing you will be confronted with when you meet Cory is his exuberance. If you are having a bad day, or if you have a physical or mental handicap, the first thing you will be met with is Cory's encouragement—because he learned something very early in life from having his particular handicap: he has the ability to reach out—to connect and comfort others who may be having a problem. He is

extremely outgoing and never hesitates to use his leg as an icebreaker if he feels that it could benefit the people around him. Let me give you an example: recently a "friend of a friend" asked Cory if he would be willing to write a short note of encouragement to a young athlete who had been in a car accident, resulting in the loss of his leg. Cory didn't hesitate. Following is a brief excerpt from the letter that he wrote to this young man:
'Hi! This is Cory. I heard you have been going through some tough times. When I was born, I was pre-mature and missing a leg, so I thought I might tell you a little bit about myself. This year I went to New York for a mission trip—I was scared, but since God has given me this leg, people thought, "look what this kid has made it through", which gave me a better chance to witness...I have a great power to witness because of my fake leg. I know that God has a plan for me and for you. I hope we are just starting God's plan for us now!'"

Did you notice how Cory sees his leg as a gift God has given him? Where most people might see a handicap, Cory sees an opening. Where others might focus on the hurdles that Cory has to overcome, he chooses to focus on the opportunities that he has been given to reach out to others, using his unique condition. His attitude not only gives him wings, but he also manages to lift those around him up to new heights as well.

> HIS ATTITUDE NOT ONLY GIVES HIM WINGS, BUT HE MANAGES TO LIFT THOSE AROUND HIM UP TO NEW HEIGHTS AS WELL.

Cory chooses to have a great attitude, so let me ask you—how's yours? I bet you have both legs. Is your attitude as good as Cory's? It can be. Let me show you how you can improve your attitude. You will never achieve your potential if your attitude is an anchor instead of a pair of wings. Remember, your attitude is always your choice. I have heard my friend John Maxwell say, "It is not what happens to you that matters but what happens *in* you that is important."

Have you noticed that most successful people have good attitudes? Author Carolyn Warner said, "I am convinced that attitude is the key to success and failure in almost any of life's endeavors." I know you want to achieve your potential, or you would never have made it this far in the book. Regardless of where your attitude is today, you can improve it. As a matter of fact, I hope your attitude will always be getting better. In God's Instruction Book, He said for you to "think like Jesus thought" (Philippians 2:5, paraphrased). He also said to "guard your heart for from it flow the issues of life" (Proverbs 4:23). Amazingly, Jesus kept an awesome attitude, even knowing of his execution on a cross. We are to do the same with our attitudes. As automotive pioneer Henry Ford said, "Whether you think you can or whether you think you can't—you're right."

> "IT IS NOT WHAT HAPPENS TO YOU THAT MATTERS BUT WHAT HAPPENS *IN* YOU THAT IS IMPORTANT."

> "WHETHER YOU THINK YOU CAN OR WHETHER YOU THINK YOU CAN'T— YOU'RE RIGHT."

Before we look at how to develop a great attitude, let me ask you a question. Do you know how bad attitudes are developed? I personally do not believe we are born with a poor attitude, do you? If you don't agree, just look at very young children, so happy and joyful and full of life. Our attitudes may turn sour, but they don't start out that way. So where does stinking thinking come from? Most of us get it pretty early in life from people we are close to, like parents, family, teachers, coaches and others. While we are young, we are like sponges. Some of what we absorb is good, the rest maybe not so much. Or we may have had early influences or training that is downright bad. Either way, this early input shapes our attitude. All of our experiences, information and examples add up to our attitude and outlook—they color our view of the world. What is terribly sad is that many people believe they are stuck with their bad attitudes, as if they were permanent conditions. WRONG!

Have you ever heard someone make excuses for a bad attitude or behavior? "Well, that's just the way I am." "My dad was just the same way." "It runs in the family." I have heard hundreds of variations of the same excuse. No matter your background, family, experiences or education, you can change your attitude if you choose. I have seen hundreds do it and their lives are better for it. Here's how:

STEP 1: Take Responsibility For Your Attitude

Please don't skim over this section; it is far too important not to read carefully. What we're going over here is not "fluff" or merely "positive thinking," and although it may sound simple, it is not at all easy. It will, however, affect your future in ways you could never imagine.

Communicator Steve Davis said, "It may not be your fault for being down, but it's got to be your fault for not getting up." You must accept responsibility; never accept excuses. In our culture few ever accept blame. "It's

> "IT MAY NOT BE YOUR FAULT FOR BEING DOWN, BUT IT'S GOT TO BE YOUR FAULT FOR NOT GETTING UP."

not my fault" is the mantra for millions. Be big! Today grow up and take charge of your attitude. If it is bad, it can be better. If it's good, it can be great.

Right now, why don't you ask my Partner for help? Ask Him to show you your attitude. Do you have any blind spots or weaknesses holding you back? Ask Him to infuse you, to inject you with a dose of awesome attitude. Everyone around you will be grateful. Your family will think a new person has moved into the house. Ask Him to show you how to think. If He's your Partner, He has big plans for you, and you will need a stellar attitude to achieve those plans. He said, "I know the plans I have for you, to give you a future and a hope" (Jeremiah 29:11). It's up to you—your choice, your responsibility. A lot of people are counting on you.

> "I KNOW THE PLANS I HAVE FOR YOU, TO GIVE YOU A FUTURE AND A HOPE."

STEP 2: Make The Decision To Be Positive

Before my feet hit the floor in the morning, my Partner and I have our first meeting. I ask Him for help to start the day—I ask for help to honor Him. A bad attitude seldom honors God. I make a choice to be positive. Sometimes I fall short. Remember, we live in a negative world. God said to walk with Him, which means we will not be going in the same direction as the rest of the world. Golfing great Arnold Palmer said his dad taught him, "Whatever game you play, 90% of success is from the shoulders up." He was right. As John Maxwell rightly said, "You are only an

> "WHATEVER GAME YOU PLAY, 90% OF SUCCESS IS FROM THE SHOULDERS UP."

attitude away from success." Either of these wise men could have been talking about you. Step two is simple—make the wise choice to be positive. Now you're ready to get started.

STEP 3: Guard Your Mind

I spend a lot of time talking to people about my Partner. Several people have accused me of being brainwashed, and I always agree with them. That shocks the ones who were looking for an argument. The truth is, we are all brainwashed on one point or another. I just choose who washes my brain. Brains are a lot like computers, and you've probably heard the term, "garbage in, garbage out." In that regard, our brains work very much like computers. Whatever you put in will come out. That's one of the reasons God warns to guard your heart and mind. Jesus Himself said what goes into your heart comes out your mouth. It usually comes out in the form of an attitude.

You may have heard the old story of the two dogs. Imagine that you have two dogs, one black and one white. If you put the white dog in the house and love, feed, and care for it, but put the black dog in the yard chained and uncared for, unfed and unloved, then the white dog will thrive while the black dog will become weak and sickly. Now if the two dogs get into a fight, which dog would win? The white dog will because he is stronger. Your attitudes and thinking patterns are much the same as the dogs. If you feed, care for and encourage your positive attitudes and thinking patterns, they will thrive. Starve your stinking thinking, and it will eventually go away. The "food" in this case includes things like TV, movies, books, magazines, friends, family, culture and so forth— whatever you take into your mind eventually finds its way into your heart and comes out in your attitude. What's influencing your attitude? If you lie down with dogs, you will come up with fleas. Choose wisely what enters your mind—it will always be there.

You may remember your parents trying to teach you some version of this lesson, but it's not just for kids. You may think you can watch, listen or participate in certain activities without any ill effects, but that's just not true. Before your attitude will improve in a lasting way, you may have to change some things: where you go, what you listen to or watch, who you hang out with and what you read.

Michele and I hadn't been married long when we moved to Memphis so I could start seminary. We lived in an apartment building with several other young couples—some were seminary students, others were not; but we were all away from home. At Thanksgiving we invited many of the couples to our apartment for dinner. Holidays can be stressful times, and several of our guests had spent most of the afternoon quarreling. Before long everybody was quarreling. After everyone left I asked Michele not to hang out with those women. I knew that if she did, eventually their attitudes would rub off, and it would adversely affect our marriage. I want to be with positive people who will help, not hinder, my marriage, ministry and life. It may sound harsh, but the fact is that you become like those you hang out with. Guard your mind. Henry Ford said, "My friends are those who bring the best out in me."

> "MY FRIENDS ARE THOSE WHO BRING THE BEST OUT IN ME."

If your childhood was anything like mine, you may have a lot of retraining to do. Much of my early input had been negative (except from my mother, of course) and needed to be changed. It requires time and effort to retrain your mind, heart and attitude. To change an attitude, you must change how you think. This is the number one reason to guard your mind and is one of the great secrets of success.

STEP 4: Add The Right Equipment

Just as a climber needs the right equipment to make a serious climb (boots, crampons, trekking poles, rope, etc.), you need the right equipment to aid your climb to your potential. Now that you have chosen to be positive and to guard your mind, you must add positive thoughts into your mind and heart. I recommend you use good CDs, books, music, seminars, friends and spend some serious time with my Positive Partner. He said, "You can do all things through Christ who strengthens you" (Philippians 4:13). He also said, "With God all things are possible" (Matthew 19:26). God Himself was and is the original positive thinker. He is the one who invented faith. We have already discussed faith. Keep working and watch it grow. In Chapter Nine I will give you some ideas on how to grow continually.

Optimist, businessman and philanthropist Clement Stone wrote, "There is little difference in people, but that little difference makes a big difference. The little difference is attitude. The big difference is whether it is positive or negative." He should know. Stone parlayed $100 into an insurance company worth millions. During his 100-year lifetime, he gave over $275 million to charity. According to the New York

> "THERE IS LITTLE DIFFERENCE IN PEOPLE, BUT THAT LITTLE DIFFERENCE MAKES A BIG DIFFERENCE. THE LITTLE DIFFERENCE IS ATTITUDE."

Times, he began each day declaring, "I feel happy, I feel healthy! I feel terrific!" And he insisted his employees do the same.

It is unbelievable how few people really work on their attitude, especially when it is so important in every area of life.

STEP 5: Enlist An Attitude Observer

I call this an accountability partner. It's someone close to you, whom you see often. They must be positive, have a commitment to help you grow, and be willing to point out when your attitude lags. Ask this person to keep an eye on you as an attitude observer. You could do the same in return. Exchange books, CDs or ideas on how to grow. Encourage each other when circumstances get difficult. I could have Cory write you a card! An attitude observer of mine sent me this quotation by author and pastor Chuck Swindoll:

> "The longer I live, the more I realize the impact of attitude on life. Attitude, to me, is more important than facts. It is more important than the past, than education, than money, than circumstances, than failures, than successes, than what other people think or say or do. It is more important than appearances, giftedness or skill. It will make or break a company...a church...a home. The remarkable thing is we have a choice every day regarding the attitude we will embrace for the day. We cannot change our past...we cannot change the fact that people will act in a certain way. We cannot change the inevitable. The only thing we can do is play on the same string we have, and that is our attitude...I am convinced that life is 10% what happens to me and 90% how I react to it. And so it is with you...we are in charge of our attitudes."

Act like the person you want to become in your attitude. It is far easier to think your way into feeling than to feel your way into thinking.

STEP 6: Never Expect To Arrive

Your attitude is a work in progress. Some days you seem to master it, and others you seem to fall ten steps back. You will always have to pay close attention to your attitude. Many people let up when they arrive at their desired position on the peak. Some let up when they become senior adults. I have heard many seniors say

> ACT LIKE THE PERSON YOU WANT TO BECOME IN ATTITUDE. IT IS FAR EASIER TO THINK YOUR WAY INTO FEELING THAN TO FEEL YOUR WAY INTO THINKING.

they are too old to worry about what they say. Age is not a license to hurt people's feelings. This leads to negativity any time we quit worrying about our attitude. Don't die before you're dead. I want to live until I die. I want to grow every day of my life. I will keep adding value to others and helping people achieve their dreams and potential up to the moment my Partner calls me home. Until then, I will help people. I get so much joy out of watching people grow and really connect with my Partner. My soul experiences joy and ecstasy of which this world knows little. This lifestyle goes against the flow of our culture, so the minute we stop paddling we begin to drift backwards.

I am always amazed at how quickly educated people "foofoo" positive thinking and attitude adjustments. Many act like the topics are for simpletons who need everything candy-coated. I feel sorry for their families and friends. Positive thinking and a great attitude cannot make you something you're not. They will not allow you to do more than you are capable of doing or accomplish more that you're able. But one thing is for sure: if your attitude is poor and your thinking is faulty, your potential will be severely limited regardless of your ability or education.

Let me share with you an amazing story I heard years ago, because your thinking could save your life—it did for Jerry. This guy was an eternal optimist. His philosophy of life was quite simple…"Each morning I wake up to two choices. I can choose to be in a good mood or a bad mood." As he frequently said, "The bottom line is, it's your choice how you live life." Jerry had the opportunity to live out that philosophy on the most difficult level. He was in the restaurant business when three armed men robbed and shot him. While lying on the restaurant floor in a pool of blood, he said, "I remembered that I had two choices: I could choose to live, or I could choose to die. I chose to live." That choice seemed to be in jeopardy, though, when he saw the faces of those in the emergency room. He recalled how all of the attending medical team seemed to look at him as a man with no hope for survival. At that point he decided he must do something fast. He immediately seized an opportunistic moment while a big, burly nurse was shouting questions at him. When she asked if he was allergic to anything, Jerry replied, "Yes." His response got the attention of everyone in the room. He took a deep breath and yelled, "*Bullets*!" As the doctors and nurses started laughing, Jerry said, "I am choosing to live. Operate on me as if I am alive, not dead." Jerry survived the experience and was soon giving his normal response to the question, "How are you?" "If I were any better, I'd be twins!" A positive attitude can't always save your life, but it sure can improve whatever life you've been given. Just ask Jerry. Jerry's attitude gave him wings to soar, even in a life or death situation. Does your attitude give you wings to soar to new heights? So many people I have met have attitudes that are anchors holding them down—tethering them to a dreamless, visionless life, destined never to achieve the potential put in them by their Creator.

I pray my Partner, God, will open your eyes to grow your attitude. I pray you see the opportunities and the bright side of every situation, like Jerry and Cory. God, help them remember and use Your words in this chapter. Today will be a great day, God. Thanks.

EIGHT

Which Peak Has the Pri$e?

Imagine you're a reporter and you're stationed at the highest peak on the mountain range. Your job is to interview those who make it—those who climb to the highest potential possible. What will these people have gained? What's waiting for them at the top? It's not always a pot of gold. Some of the richest and most successful people on earth have very little money. Does this surprise you? Let's at least consider the possibilities for a moment. Think about it. Just how much does money really matter in the end? How much do you have to have to be happy? As many financially wealthy people have shared with me: "Just a little more than I have right now."

I remember a really hectic time for Michele and me. I was not only in finals; but both my jobs were requiring a great deal of time, and Michele's was also. As usual, the money ran out before the month did. (I'm sure you've NEVER experienced anything like

99

that.) Michele was working as a bank teller, and I was a full-time student and part-time Associate Pastor working with youth. I was also laying carpet on the side to make ends meet. Even with all three jobs our household income was less than 20K. Our daughter Faith had just been born, and we were having a hard time making it. The cold winter meant the electric bill was higher than normal. Even with all this stuff going on, our family had enjoyed a great Sunday at church, and we were headed to the car to go home. Michele and I had both prayed for the Lord to provide for us since we didn't have any food at home—we were completely broke. The bills had been piling up, which was normal. Being poor usually wasn't that bad, just a little inconvenient. When we got out to the car to drive home, we found the back seat was full of groceries! We put Faith into her car seat and cried with relief and joy all the way home. Once again, our Partner had provided. We were having the time of our lives.

So the question is still on the table: how much does money really matter in the end? How many zeros does it take to be happy or successful? If we hadn't had the dire need from being broke in the first place, God never would have been able to bless us with His provision. We learned many lessons about faith in those days of being broke. If you don't have a problem, then you don't need a miracle.

I could tell you stories all day of how God has come through for us so many times and in so many ways. Michele and I spent the first half of our marriage without much money, which is quite typical of people starting a marriage, family, school or a new career. Thankfully our net-worth does not equal our self-worth. Our value to God has nothing to do with our "bottom line."

Mary had no money, yet God picked her to carry the Baby Jesus because she had found favor with Him. Many of the people God chose in the Bible (and still chooses today) to use in mighty ways were not financially well-off. Your personal value has nothing to do with the amount of money you've accumulated. Some people will amass a great deal of wealth and still not achieve their potential; others like Mother Teresa will touch the world without making any real money at all.

Achieving your full potential does not by any stretch of the imagination mean you must have a lot of money. Since being financially wealthy is limited to a small segment of the world's population, your success and your potential are far more than money. Sadly, too many people equate success with climbing the corporate ladder or having a huge bank account. Ask some of the rich if they feel successful. Many will say no. You can have money and still have a hole in your heart. I have had the opportunity to minister to many wealthy people. They have the same heartaches, needs and longings as those without money. I have had more than one person tell me they would give all the money they had to have their spouse back, kids back or just a chance to do it all over again. Finances are great, but if they are your only standard of success, you've shortchanged yourself. I have been around the world and seen some successful happy people, yet they don't have much money. The only thing money provides is options. As a matter of fact, rich people can sometimes be more messed up than most.

There is a man in our church named Michael Dunn who has Downs Syndrome. He will never make much money, but he has a smile that will light up the room. Every Sunday Michael brings me my "paperwork," a few pages of the Bible he has copied off his computer. Michael has worked as a greeter and helps pass out worship folders. His wife is also a very special lady. She has worked in our infant nursery for over ten years. They will never be rich, but they give their all for God and serve His church to the best of their ability. Both Michael and Karen hold down 40-hour-a-week jobs and are working hard to achieve their full potential. Surprisingly, they live alone in a home they pay for and even take care of some of their own personal business. Michael's parents live nearby and help out. Their worth has nothing to do with their wealth. I believe they are achieving their full potential, and God is always there to help them. Today in Harriman, Tennessee, there is a school for the mentally challenged named in Michael's honor.

One of the problems with riches and great abilities is that you will be held to a higher standard. God said, "To whom much is given, much is required" (Luke 12:48). That means people with many talents, abilities and wealth are expected to accomplish more, and that can distract from what the real priorities are in life. As a matter of fact, Jesus said it is "easier for a camel to go through the eye of a needle than for a rich man to enter the kingdom of heaven" (Matthew 19:24). That's pretty strong language.

Money is a great tool, and it opens many doors. Usually, as you grow in your chosen field, you can make more money. It's okay to make money. Remember another "Partner Principle:" "The love of money is the root of all sorts of evil" (1 Timothy 6:10). Please don't be side-tracked in the pursuit of your potential and fall into the trap of thinking money is the "end all" of everything. It is not. You can use money, or money can use you. You can fulfill your potential and never acquire a pile of money. Abraham is called the father of faith. He did one thing that changed the world. He had a son named Isaac. He fulfilled his potential and changed the world through his son.

What is your potential? How far can you go? These are far better questions than how much money you make or what you have in the bank.

Let me tell you four things money is not. First, money is not a measure of your success. Second, money is not a component of your self-worth. Next, money is not necessarily a reward for spiritual living. And last, money is not a guarantee of your satisfaction in life. I feel the need to repeat this thought about success over and over again because our culture has drilled it into our heads that money is the equivalent of success. Between Hollywood and Wall Street, most Americans believe if they do not have the right house, car, clothes and cologne that they cannot be happy or successful. This could not be further from the truth.

I love what motivational speaker Zig Ziglar said, "I like the things that money can buy; I'll bet you do, too. I like nice clothes, a beautiful residence, big, comfortable cars, relaxing vacations, membership in a nice country club and so on. However, I love the things money won't buy. It will buy me a house, but not a home; a bed, but not a good night's sleep; pleasure, but not happiness; a good time, but not peace of mind; and a companion, but not a friend." Zig is so right. All the important things in life can't be bought: love, friendship, family, health, peace, joy, victory, clear conscience and the list goes on.

I have many friends, some who are rich and some who are poor—financially anyway. Money does not give my wealthy friends any more happiness or success than the ones without money. Many of my friends without much money are very successful in life and are reaching their full potential. As a matter of fact, having a lot of money would probably get in their way. Look at all the people that win the lottery—many of them are ruined.

I have a friend named Terry duPont who lives in Costa Rica, Central America. Terry was a hospital administrator in Knoxville. He was a very successful executive and enjoyed all the frills money brought. Terry met God when he was in his mid-forties, and left the executive world for a world of helping people spiritually. He founded the church where I am now pastor. After several years of successful church work, he felt his Partner was asking him to move to Central America. Terry and his wife Arlene sold their beautiful Cape Cod-style home and all their possessions and moved out of the country. Terry was in his early sixties and did not know a word of Spanish at the time. They had little support from their family and even less financial support.

I've been down to Central America many times with Terry and Arlene. It is amazing to see the tens of thousands of lives they have touched though their Open Eyes Ministries (www.openeyes.org). They started in Nicaragua, expanded to Honduras, then to Costa Rica and plan to continue the expansion into El Salvador. Few gave them hope of making it. After all, they had no experience and no training...but they had a vision from their Partner, and look at them today!

Do they have much money? No, but they support a staff of over 100. They provide for hundreds of orphans, homeless and hungry. Hundreds of Americans go for a week every year to help in their great work. Money? No. Friends? Yes. Excitement? Yes. Faith? Yes. Victory? Yes. Miracles? You bet, and the sure knowledge they are achieving their full potential for their unseen Partner. I personally have seen few climb so high.

Your value has nothing to do with what's in your checkbook or your bank account but what is in your heart. Success is about loving your family, adding value to others, experiencing exciting relationships and achieving your potential. When I die, they will bury me and then throw dirt on me. Everyone will go back to the church and eat potato salad. What will they say? I will consider my life a success if my wife knows how much I loved her and says I was "the best husband in the world," if my three kids say "my dad loved me and was my best friend, and my dad loved God." I hope the church will be full of people I helped connect with God and discover their potential. Then I will have been a success. I will spend my life to make this happen, and I believe my Partner will be happy with me, and I'll hear the words, "Well done faithful servant" (Matthew 25:21).

> IF YOUR SUMMIT IS SILVER AND YOUR GOD IS GOLD—YOU DON'T HAVE TO CLIMB VERY HIGH.

This kind of life I've described money can't buy. If your summit is silver and your god is gold—you don't have to climb very high. How much higher did Jesus Christ climb past profit? If money is the mark of success, I guess He was a failure!

No, money is not the measure of success. If it were, the old joke would be true that "he who dies with the most toys wins." I believe the ones with the most friends win. Relationships really win. At the peak of your potential are people—people who love and care about you.

We've all heard it said that the streets of heaven are made of gold. How shocked must the angels be when so many of us spend our entire lives working for asphalt!

NINE

Strategies for the Summit

The dark walnut-paneled room was full of seminary professors surrounding a conference table that was large and looming. All of the men sat in high-back leather chairs with their critically discerning eyes on me. It was the day of reckoning. This group would decide whether or not I would be accepted into the doctoral program of the New Orleans Baptist Theological Seminary. Needless to say, I was a bit nervous. Boy, was this a long way from the projects in Chattanooga!

It had taken months of work to get to this interview. I had read books, written reports and taken a battery of tests, including IQ tests, stress tests and personality tests. I had answered questionnaires and filled out unending numbers of papers and forms. All of this was just to get in the door, into the program. I could understand if it were during the course, in order to graduate, but just to get in—this seemed ridiculous. But there I was, nerves and all.

I will always remember this inquiry from the educators. The last question the group asked was, "Chris, it says here you read two books a week; is this true?" "Yes, sir," I responded. "Well, that is very strange. Most people who graduate with their Master's seldom read again."

To me that was inconceivable. How can people stop reading and learning after school? Do people read in school just to get out or actually to learn? At this point in my ministry, I realized most people don't have a personal growth plan. I had assumed earlier that most educated people, especially those involved in leading people, had such plans. Not so. But every climber must prepare and plan if they are to keep climbing. Personal growth never just happens. It requires a plan of action and a great deal of effort. The reason mountain climbers are viewed with great respect is because of how hard it is to climb. We all recognize at least part of the difficulty and danger of climbing the world's highest mountains. It is the same with achieving your potential. It's just hard; that's the reason so few actually accomplish the feat. You can't just sit in front of the TV and grow emotionally, intellectually, professionally, spiritually or any other way.

> EVERY CLIMBER MUST PREPARE AND PLAN IF THEY ARE TO KEEP CLIMBING.

What about you—do you have a growth plan? If you are going to reach your full potential, you must develop a plan for your continual growth and improvement. Great mentors I have had like John Maxwell have instilled in me a passion for personal growth. One of Israel's greatest kings prayed, "Lord, sustain me with a willing spirit" (Psalm 51:12b). Basically he was asking God to make him "want to" desire to remain faithful. Ask my Partner to give you a passion, a strong desire to want to grow. The day you stop growing is the day you stop moving higher toward your potential. As you have heard many times, "If you fail to plan, you plan to fail." Your growth and potential are far too important to leave to chance. In the rest of this chapter I hope to give you some great ideas for your Personal Growth Plan (PGP).

You can imagine that in my line of work December is a very busy month. There is so much preparation for the Christmas season: plans, parties, programs, pageants, worship events and so forth. Then as quickly as the fury arises, it subsides. For the two weeks around Christmas and New Year's Day there is nothing— dead time. I love that time of the year. As I write this chapter I am just starting that period. With some additional free time, I try to use it to the fullest. My Partner said to "make the best use of time" (Ephesians 5:16). There are two important things I do that have a direct bearing on my PGP.

The first thing I do is evaluate the year that's winding down. I take my calendar and spend some time looking back over the great victories as well as the failures. I look for what gave me wings and what weighed me down, my anchors. This tells me what I should do again and what to omit from my schedule next time around. I also review my personal goals and my PGP. Did I achieve my goals? Did I stay on track with my growth plan? This is an invaluable experience because it allows time for my Partner to speak to me. You must review and evaluate your experiences if you expect to grow from them.

The second thing I do during this time frame is to lay out my PGP and goals for the New Year. By this time I've been praying for at least two months about my goals, and I'll use last year's growth plan to start forming the new one. Notes from throughout the year in my prayer journal also help in crafting these important documents for my future growth. Now it's time to meet with my Partner to see exactly how to finish the new goals and PGP. By this time I'm very excited about the New Year. I'm looking forward to miracles, great growth, and fresh vision, experiences and views from new vistas yet to be reached.

The goals and plan will complement each other. After all, you can't expect to reach a goal of playing for the NBA if all you ever plan to do is shoot hoops in the backyard. Your plan and goals should be different from anyone else's—they will be as unique as you are. So while I invite you to follow my process, your goals and plan will be your own. Now remember, I'm a teacher-communicator and leader for thousands. That means my number one focus in my PGP is spending time with my Partner. I set aside approximately two hours a day for meeting with Him. It's the most important thing I do. I can't imagine anyone having something that's more important. Just as I set a certain amount of time for the Master daily, I hope your plan reflects quality time with God.

It's also very important to give God the best part of your day. Many people think that to be close to God, they have to get up early in the morning, but some people are just not morning people. So they might get up but then keep falling asleep on God. Don't do that. Give God your best part. If you're a morning person, give God time early in the morning. If you are a late-night person, set that time for the Lord. Maybe the afternoon is your best—then set time in the afternoon for Him.

All of the traditional spiritual disciplines should be reflected in your PGP. In case you're not familiar with them, I've listed some of them here:

- Time in the Owner's Manual (Bible).
  A systematic approach is best, not the drop-flop method. This means dropping the Bible and reading wherever it flops open. Not the best method!
- Scripture memory
- Meditation on the Bible
- Prayer
- Fasting
- Reading other books: Christian, leadership, family...
- Sharing your faith
- Ministry in your local church and community
- Small Group involvement for community
- Observing the Sabbath
- Silence
- Solitude
- Journaling

Your spiritual life is much like your physical life; you must work out or exercise yourself spiritually (as well as physically), using a variety of activities if you expect to achieve and maintain total health. Look at how you can use the disciplines listed above.

Look at your calendar and set aside time. Block it off, and don't let anything interfere. For you to grow, you must put forth an effort. This is how you do it. It will positively affect every area of your life.

Set goals that you can reach but that will also make you stretch. If your plan is not attainable, change it so you can reach it! After you have completed your PGP, give it to someone to hold you accountable. Now it is also the time for you to set goals for the year. Your goals should be not only spiritual but physical as well. For example:

- How many books will you read this year?
- What CDs will you listen to? (The car is a great place to learn—use that time!)
- With how many people will you share your faith?
- How much of the Bible will you read? (Maybe read it through in one year—it only takes three chapters a day!)
- How many verses will you memorize?
- How much time will you spend with your spouse?
- How much time with your kids?
- How much money will you save?
- How much money will you give?
- Any other financial planning?
- Will you go to any seminars, retreats, or conferences?
- Any professional training?
- Any degrees you need to complete?
- What about promotions or job-related goals?
- Do you have any physical fitness goals? How will you reach them?
- Where does God want you to be at the end of the year?

These are just a few of the questions you should ask yourself in designing your goals for the year. Some of the goals may take longer than a year, but designate some things to do now toward those goals. The time you spend with God will give you insight into all the ideas above. When you sit down and spend time with Him I would encourage you to listen with a pen and paper in hand. Take notes and use them in formulating your plans. Sadly, the business of our society today feeds our egos and starves our souls. You may feel you're too busy, but I assure you that time well spent with your Partner will refresh your spirit and prepare you to win the battles ahead. If you do this for a few years, not only will it get easier, but you will go farther and higher than you ever imagined.

One of my long-range goals was to have my doctorate before I was 40. I was on track to complete it until I came to my last two weeks of scheduled time on campus, for the professional writer's seminar. For some reason I didn't receive a packet of work I was to have done before I arrived.

I was in my seat bright and early on Monday morning the first day. After a few pleasantries the professor asked for the work to be handed in. You can imagine my shock as I saw the other students handing in reams of work all completed. During the lunch break the professor asked to speak with me. He asked about my missing assignments. I explained, but he told me I couldn't finish the work and should just go home. He said it was not a big deal, I could just sign up for the class again in June. But that was unacceptable to me. I had set my long range goals to finish my doctorate before I was 40. If I left, I could not graduate by July, when I would turn 40.

I told the professor I would be back to his office by Thursday morning at 8:00 a.m. with all the work completed. He assured me that would be impossible but agreed that I could try. Thursday at 8:00 I handed in all the work. The professor couldn't believe it, but I knew I had a plan and to keep up with it I had to get the work done. If I had not had the plan, I would have put it off for another year. Instead, I graduated in May of that year, two months before I turned 40. That's just one example of the power and speed you can gain from having a clear and tangible plan.

What goals does God have for you? Get with God. Write them down and plan them out, then plan what steps you have to take to reach them. After five or ten years, just think how far God can take you.

If you are new to spending time with God, let me give you some helpful hints. When I first met God, I asked every spiritual leader I knew how they spent time with Him. I tried many ways and ideas. All of them helped me grow deeper in my new walk. It seemed everyone that was close to God had one thing in common—they spent quality time with Him. I set out on a mission to learn to do that too. Now after 24 years of growth, time with God and a PGP, I have developed a system that works for me. Maybe it will help you, too.

Every day, I spend about two hours with my powerful Partner. Usually I have the same basic agenda: I read a chapter or two from the current book I'm studying. Next, I get out my prayer journal and start with the date at the top of the page and just begin to talk to God. I write out my prayers because my mind runs at ten thousand RPMs, and it's hard for me to stay focused otherwise. By writing I can stay on track. I usually share my thoughts, questions, victories and problems with my wise Partner. After about 30 minutes I open my Bible and begin reading according to my current study plan. After reading I go back to my journal to record my thoughts, leadings, and meditations from the Scriptures. Next, I pray for my church; I pray in faith for God's strong hand to move. Using meditation and visualization I let my mind see the great things I believe God will do and ask Him to accomplish them. After I finish praying for the church and the annual goals for the church, I pray for my family, starting with my three children. I pray about issues they're facing, who they're dating and for their future mates. I dream for them. I see God's hand of favor resting on them, and I pray for their protection and direction in their decisions. Next I pray for my wife Michele. I pray for issues she's facing and the needs in her life. I pray for our marriage and our love. I ask God to protect our marriage, family and ministry. He is so faithful to answer prayers. I also make several declarations of faith about the day.

By this time I've spent about two hours in the presence of my awesome Partner, and I am set for the day. I try not to get into a rut, so I may change my schedule somewhat. What is non-negotiable is my time with the Lord. I love Him so much and so enjoy "seeking Him with my whole heart." I believe when I see Him face to face I will hear, "Well done, good and faithful servant."

Climbers of the world's highest mountain peaks prepare for years for their ascents. They plan for the physical requirements and endurance essential to their excursions. The climbers prepare the team. They also prepare the route of the climb. Real climbers leave as little to chance as possible. What's your plan for growth and the future? Are you leaving too much to chance? I've included some ideas in Appendix One to help you in the five major areas of growth. As you read this, I am completing a second book devoted solely to helping you develop your own Personal Growth Plan.

TEN

Who Is In Command
of the Expedition?

Wow! I must say I'm impressed you've made it this far in
the book. You've probably enjoyed some of the book and had
reservations in other parts. Either way, you're to be congratulated.
I'm glad you're reading the book, but I'm most excited you're
reading this chapter because it is by far the most important. We'll
cover the single most important issue in all of our lives. You might
wonder, if it is so important, why didn't I put it at the beginning
of the book, and that would be a great question. The reason is that
some of you weren't ready for it when you started reading. That
may sound strange, so let me explain.

Every climbing expedition must have a head, a leader. Hopefully, by now it's obvious you can't go it alone. It is too far and
too difficult to achieve without help. So in your journey up the
mountain, who's in charge? This is vital because it determines
whether or not you achieve your destiny.

As you no doubt noticed throughout our time together, I've used many names for God. Most of them indicate that He heads up my expedition. He's been the Partner-in-Charge ever since my stay in the hospital. That was the day I was changed forever. You've probably heard the term "born again," but it really was as if a *new* Chris left the hospital. The main reason for the change was that I made some serious life-changing decisions. Up until then, I had completely wrecked my life. I didn't know a valley could be so low or so deep, and I could not have climbed out on my own.

Today God is my CEO, and I work for Him. As you've gotten deeper into this book, I've given you more Scriptures and more information about my Partner. Hopefully, your curiosity and interest are piqued. I said in the first chapter that I didn't have a formula for success. I still don't, but God does. He is my formula and Father.

Now it's time to get down to serious business with my Senior Partner. God wants to be your Partner, too. He longs for an intimate relationship with you. Not for you to be religious but for you to know Him. It's so sad that when many people think of God, religion automatically pops into their minds. Religion is mankind working his or her way to God. By jumping through a series of hoops or adhering to certain behaviors, you can theoretically gain God's approval. Just about every culture and civilization has had a religion. Sometimes many different religions. This is not what I'm talking about. I'm speaking to you about a personal relation-ship with God, not a religion. For many people Christianity has become a religion, and God ends up being left out of the equation. Biblical Christianity is not us working our way to God, but His rescuing of us. As a matter of fact, "He loved you so much He gave His only Son for you" (John 3:16). This is a huge issue and a BIG DEAL—you must come to God on His terms. Sound strong? He is God, and as God, He is the CEO of the universe. That means He gets to call the shots. If you are to become His partner, you must acknowledge that He is the Lord or CEO of your life and heart. He will accept no less. "That if you confess with your mouth Jesus as Lord, and believe in your heart that God raised Him from the dead, you will be saved; for with the heart a person believes, resulting in righteousness, and with the mouth he confesses, resulting in salvation" (Romans 10:9-10). This thought is hard for some because it hits us right in our pride. It establishes our need for God, and most of us erroneously think we can climb by ourselves.

Please forgive me if some of this language sounds religious because it's not. God is no fan of religion. Many people hear the word *Bible* and they think religion and shut down without ever knowing what God has done for us. He said pure religion was to "take care of widows and orphans and keep yourself unstained by the world" (James 1:27). Remember, from a biblical standpoint, most of what masquerades as religion is man-made and contrived. The whole Bible is about a relationship between you and God. On His terms, of course. Most people look at those who go to church and say they are religious. But not everyone that goes to church has a relationship with the God of the universe. Do you have a relationship with Him?

The truth remains that He is God, and He made us in His image. We did not make God in our image. There are not many roads to God—just one. He made the road. Jesus said, "You must be born again" (John 3:3). This is not an option or just a good idea; He said it was the only way anyone would see heaven. My Partner has been very clear in the Scripture about how to meet Him and become His partner. He did not say the way to Him was religion. Many people try many ways to get to God and act as if it's up to them instead of God to develop the process! Again, remember He is God, and as God, He gets to call all the shots. Let me give you the steps He has laid out for us in His Word, the *Ultimate Climbing Guide*:

1. Realize You Are Separated From God By Your Sin.

You may or may not think you've lived a pretty good life, but God says, "we have all sinned" (Romans 3:23). If you have ever lied, cheated, lusted, been angry, taken God's name in vain or stolen anything, then you have broken the Big Ten (Ten Commandments). You've sinned. Period. Big or little doesn't matter. This "Partner Principle" is found all through the Bible. Isaiah said, "Your sins have hidden God's face from you; you have been separated from Him" (Isaiah 59:2, paraphrased). Let's get real. We've all sinned and missed the mark of perfection. God is still perfect and demands a payment for sin...a debt we can never fulfill on our own. Do you have rules at your house that result in automatic punishment when they're broken? So does God.

When my kids were young, lying carried an automatic penalty—spanking! My middle child, Micah, was about three or four years old. He and I were alone for the evening and were having a good time when out of the blue, he told me a lie. I was sad because we both knew the tone of the evening had to change. He knew the punishment. I took him to my room for the unpleasant task. As

Micah bent over the bed he heard three whacks, but he didn't feel anything. He looked up at me with a puzzled expression. Then he saw three red marks on my legs. "Why?" he asked. "Micah, you lied, and the punishment must be given. I love you so I took your spanking for you," I then went on to tell him how Jesus took our spanking, how He paid for our sins on the cross.

2. Confess That You Have Sinned.

To confess means to agree with God. He already knows you've sinned, so you won't shock God. You and I must drop our pride and tell God we've blown it, and we know it. For most of us, it's hard to say we were wrong. Pride will keep many people away from God. I hope and pray you are not one of them.

3. Accept The Free Gift.

Next is realizing God said the "payment of sin is death" and that is what we all deserve. "But the free gift of God is eternal life" (Romans 6:23). Just as I took the spanking my son deserved, Jesus has paid the price for our sin. Wow—is that good news! In reality this is a business transaction in the spiritual world, and you get the better end of the deal. God forgives our sin and gives us a fresh new start.

> IN REALITY THIS IS A BUSINESS TRANSACTION IN THE SPIRITUAL WORLD, AND YOU GET THE BETTER END OF THE DEAL.

Then He becomes the CEO of our lives and blesses our socks off. How much better can you get?

"But God demonstrates His own love toward us, in that while we were yet sinners, Christ died for us" (Romans 5:8). Remember, God is just and can't overlook sin. Are you ready for the transaction and the transformation? Oh yeah, you get a new heart full of love, too. The deal just gets better and better. Now we get to the time of choice, if you are ready to make the deal.

4. Answer The Door.

Revelation 3:20 says, "Behold I stand at the door and knock; if anyone hears my voice and opens the door, I will come in to him and dine with him and he with me." Jesus stands at the door of your heart and knocks. Do you hear it? He has been knocking for some time now. It's time to open the door. Ask Him to come in. Tell Him you've sinned and want to be forgiven. You want Him to be your Lord—CEO. Tell Him you believe He was born on Christmas and died on a cross; that He rose from the grave on Easter and is alive today and that you gladly confess Him as the new Director of your life and heart. This is not as easy as it may sound. Relinquishing rule of your heart can be rough. The bottom line is, who will be in charge of your life, you or God? I'm convinced He does a better job. My life is a testimony and trophy of His grace.

5. Pray.

By faith, pray this prayer with me: "Dear Jesus, I know I have sinned and broken your laws. I am sorry. Please forgive me. I ask you to come into my heart and be my Lord. I know you died for me and rose from the grave on Easter. Thank you. Teach me to live for you. I give you total control and acknowledge you are the boss of my life. Thank you for hearing me and changing me. I will live for you because you died for me. In the Name of Jesus." (Romans 10:13 says, "Whoever calls on the name of the Lord will be saved.")

6. Party With Heaven!

Now the angels in heaven are having a party. Jesus said, "When one sinner turns to him, there is a party in heaven" (Luke 15:10, paraphrased). This party is for you in your honor.

7. Find A Church.

Now it's time to find a good church in which to learn, grow and worship. You may be like I was, not having grown up in church; well, it's time to start because the Boss said so. Remember, He is now your CEO, and as the Senior Partner, He calls the shots. Never forget His plans are the best. He can think way bigger than you and I can.

8. Tell Me About It.

Please e-mail or write me so I can rejoice with you. You can look me up at www.DrChrisStephens.com or www.faithpromise. org. There you will find teaching and daily devotional thoughts to help you on your amazing new journey. Your Partner said, "I know the plans I have for you, plans to give you a future and a hope" (Jeremiah 29:11). I have talked to thousands of people about their relationship with God. I have never met anyone who regretted walking with the Lord, but I have met many who regretted ignoring God. Where do you fall? Please don't finish this life and miss God.

9. Tell Others, Too.

You may know people who need this book. Please give it to them or buy them a copy. Believe me that if God can pull me out of the pit, He can do it for you or anyone.

I can't wait to see how high you soar!

ELEVEN

The Climb Ends Here: Beyond the Summit

"You know, Chris, all this mountain climbing sounds great, but I think I've climbed high enough. Why shouldn't I just enjoy the view from the peaceful perch I've gotten to? What does it matter? Is it any big deal if I don't achieve my potential? Who really cares in the end?" These are great questions that are asked regularly. Most people don't like to think about them this way, but they deal with death. Think about it. If you're not moving forward, you're going back, right? And if you work for a company with a CEO, you're accountable to that person or his or her designee. Like employees during annual review time, as creations of God, we will all stand accountable before Him one day. Romans 14:12 says, "So then each one of us will all give an account of himself to God."

> WHAT DOES IT MATTER? IS IT ANY BIG DEAL IF I DON'T ACHIEVE MY POTENTIAL? WHO REALLY CARES IN THE END?

This thought is not a new one. God told the first man, Adam, to take care of His world for Him. (See Genesis 1:28) All through the Scriptures we are told to prepare to stand before the Judge of the universe. I could list for you literally hundreds of verses that reveal our accountability to God. Our stewardship (that is, caretaking for the Boss) is a common theme throughout the Bible.

You and I live in a world where we try to prepare for the future. We have insurance, 401Ks, annuities, portfolios and plans for retirement. Most Americans spend quite a bit of time contemplating how they will live out their retirement and how they will fare financially. These are great concerns and should have our attention, but please tell me why we give so much thought to our twilight years and so little to our eternity? Too many people give no thought to being held accountable for all they've been given. We show our gratitude in how we measure up to the gift of our potential. Again, it's great if we are going to prepare for retirement, but shouldn't we focus even more on forever?

Romans 14:12 is clear that we will give an "account to God." Since the Bible is very plain on this topic, let me give you a few things that will help you. The first one we covered in Chapter Ten, about making God your CEO. You must have a relationship with the God of the universe through His Son, Jesus. This is non-negotiable. One other issue is also very clear: as we stand to give an account, we will be measured by our potential—the gifts and talents God has given each one of us. What did we do with them? Jesus used a parable on this subject while teaching His Disciples. It's called the parable of the talents. You can find the story in Matthew 25:14-30. Basically, the Land Owner (God) gives his servants (us) some talents. These talents were amounts of money, specific weights of silver to be used for investment until the owner returned. He gave one servant five, one servant two and to the other he gave only one. He said he gave the talents according to each of their abilities. Upon his return he called for an account from his servants. Remember, the Owner has that right, to ask, "What did you do with what I gave you? I asked you to take good care of it for me."

The first servant came up to him with all smiles. "You gave me five talents and here, I have doubled them for you," and gave the Owner ten. "Well done; you will be ruler over ten cities." The next servant also came up to the Owner smiling. "You gave me two talents. Here, I doubled them to four." Again the Master was well-pleased and gave the same praise and reward. The last servant came up slowly. "I knew you were a harsh man, so I hid your talent in the ground. Here, have what was yours." People often erroneously read this and characterize God as being mean or vindictive. Most dismiss the fact that God had just given away fourteen cities and almost one hundred-fifty pounds of silver.

But in the story the Master was angry with the lazy servant. He was upset because the servant misused what the Master had given him. He took the talent away from him and gave it to the one who had ten. He then sent the servant out to be punished. The Land Owner is God. The talents are representative of gifts and abilities God has given us. They represent our potential. Those who use what God gives them will be rewarded, praised and given even more. Those who do not use or appreciate what they have been given are going to face an unhappy Lord. Remember, He is God and as such, has all rights and authority.

How do you feel when your kids don't live up to what you know is their potential? Are you happy when your exceptionally bright child comes home with D's or F's when you know that he or she is capable of making A's? It is the same with God.

One day you will stand before God. How will you fare? He has given us all we need in His Word to prepare for that day. "But Chris, I don't believe that God would ever judge anyone." Are you sure? Are you ready to bet your forever? Because that is exactly what you are doing.

> "BUT CHRIS, I DON'T BELIEVE THAT GOD WOULD EVER JUDGE ANYONE." ARE YOU SURE? ARE YOU READY TO BET YOUR FOREVER?

I wrote this book because I care. I have really struggled with writing it, but my Partner won out. He put this book into your hands to give you another chance. He loves you and wants you to be ready for heaven and to have a great life here, too. I am a satisfied customer! God has blessed me beyond belief; I would have never dreamed my life would be this great, nor did I ever dream God would use me at all. I was just a used-up drug dealer, but He is, after all, God. If God can change my life and use me, just think of what He can do in and through you. "Eye has not seen nor has ear heard what God has prepared for those who love Him" (1 Corinthians 2:9). I can't wait!

The view gets so much better the higher you climb! Trust me; I've been lower than the bottom of the valley. I never dreamed I would see the heights, and if I can, so can you! It's time to start climbing!

P.S. If this book has been helpful to you, please post a review on my website, www.DrChrisStephens.com. Your comments will be used to help fellow climbers on the mountain.

Personal Growth Plan for: _____

FAITH

Quantify the spiritual disciplines below so you can measure them. Some can be measured by amount and others by a set amount of time. Please don't omit the ones you don't enjoy—like fasting!

Bible Reading: _____
pages or chapters

Bible Study: _____
time

Scripture Memory: _____
# of verses

Meditation: _____
time

Silence: _____
time

Solitude: _____
time

Prayer: _____
time

Fasting: _____
# of days or meals

Evangelism: _____
# of people

Extra Books Read: _____
# of books

CDs, DVDs or Podcasts: _____
listened to

Serving: _____
time

List areas that need improvement or attention:

_____

_____

_____

_____

_____

Set goals or make plans for all of the above.

FAMILY

Family Time(s): _____

_____

Family Dinners: _____

_____

Family Vacations: _____

Family Devotionals: _____

Spouse Date(s): _____

Once you set the goals, put them on your calendar. Guard the time, for you will never get it back!

Projects: _____

Hobbies: _____

FITNESS

Fitness: _____

Weight: _____Maintain

_____Loss

_____Gain

Exercise: _____

_____

FORTUNE

I would encourage you to go to Dave Ramsey's website www.DaveRamsey.com. You can print several sheets to aid in budgeting, planning and envisioning your financial future. Another good site is www.crown.org.

Give: _____%

Save: _____%

Invest: _____%

Budget and Living Expenses:

_____

_____

Set Goals: _____

Develop a Plan: _____

Discipline Daily: _____

FUTURE

Education: _____

Career Path: _____

Plan to pursue your passion!

About the Author

A gifted communicator who easily connects with others, Dr. Chris Stephens uses his unique experience and relevant teaching style to touch the hearts of every age group. Since joining Faith Promise Church as Senior Pastor in July 1996, Chris has been instrumental in facilitating the church's growth from 250 to almost 3,000 in attendance, and building a staff that has grown from 5 to 40. He has a genuine passion to encourage, inspire and equip others to discover and use their God-given gifts, finding and fulfilling the purpose for their lives in the process.

Chris graduated with a Bachelor of Science from the University of Tennessee at Chattanooga, a Master of Divinity from Mid-America Baptist Theological Seminary and a Doctor of Ministry in Evangelistic Church Growth from New Orleans Baptist Theological Seminary. Dr. John Maxwell, founder of EQUIP and INJOY Stewardship Services, named Chris one of the *Top 40 Young Leaders in America*.

Chris and Michele, his wife of 24 years, live in Knoxville, Tennessee. They have three children—Faith, Micah and Zac.

"We proclaim Him, admonishing every man and teaching every man with all wisdom, so that we may present every man complete in Christ. For this purpose also I labor, striving according to His power, which mightily works within me."
Colossians 1:28-29

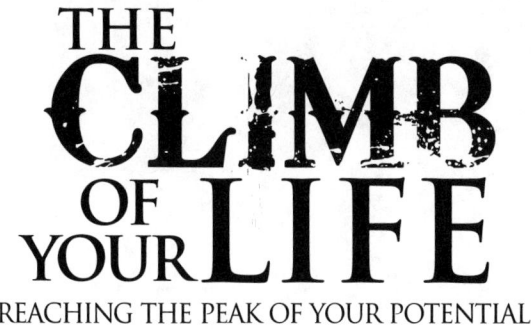

THE
CLIMB
OF LIFE
YOUR
REACHING THE PEAK OF YOUR POTENTIAL

Order additional copies of
The Climb of Your Life

www.DrChrisStephens.com

Faith Promise Church
10740 Faith Promise Lane
Knoxville, TN 37931
865-251-2590
www.faithpromise.org

NOTES

NOTES

NOTES